INTRODUCING

Darwin
and Evolution

Jonathan Miller and Borin Van Loon

Edited by Richard Appignanesi

ICON BOOKS UK   TOTEM BOOKS USA

This edition published in the UK
in 2000 by Icon Books Ltd.,
Grange Road, Duxford,
Cambridge CB2 4QF
email: icon@mistral.co.uk
www.iconbooks.co.uk

First published in the United States
in 2000 by Totem Books
Inquiries to: PO Box 223,
Canal Street Station,
New York, NY 10013

Distributed in the UK, Europe,
Canada, South Africa and Asia by the
Penguin Group: Penguin Books Ltd.,
27 Wrights Lane, London W8 5TZ

In the United States,
distributed to the trade by
National Book Network Inc.,
4720 Boston Way, Lanham,
Maryland 20706

This edition published in Australia
in 2000 by Allen & Unwin Pty. Ltd.,
PO Box 8500, 9 Atchison Street,
St. Leonards NSW 2065

Previously published in the UK in 1992
and Australia in 1994 under the title
Darwin for Beginners

Reprinted 1993, 1994, 1995, 1996

Originating editor: Richard Appignanesi

Printed and bound in Australia
by McPherson's Printing Group, Victoria

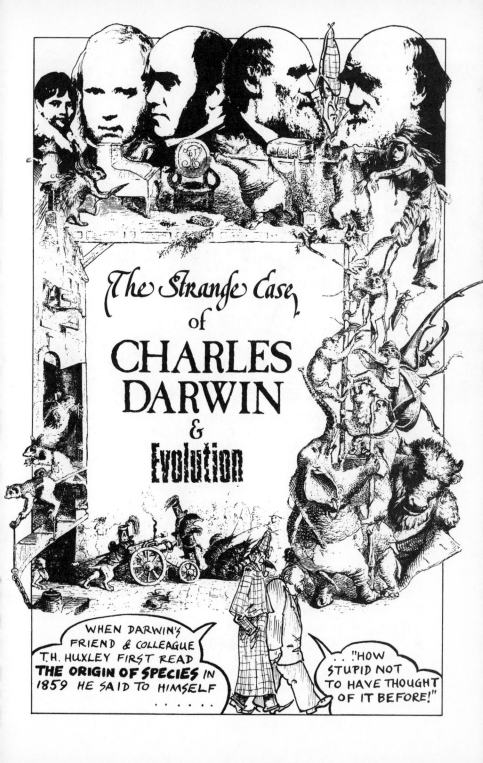

The Strange Case of

CHARLES DARWIN

&

Evolution

WHEN DARWIN'S FRIEND & COLLEAGUE T.H. HUXLEY FIRST READ **THE ORIGIN OF SPECIES** IN 1859 HE SAID TO HIMSELF . . . . . .

. . ."HOW STUPID NOT TO HAVE THOUGHT OF IT BEFORE!"

HUXLEY WAS OVERWHELMED BY ITS REVOLUTIONARY IMPORTANCE & DEVOTED SO MUCH OF HIS LIFE TO DEFENDING & POPULARIZING THE THEORY OF DESCENT WITH MODIFICATION THAT HE EARNED THE NAME OF...

DARWIN'S BULLDOG.

AND YET FOR A MAJOR WORK OF SCIENTIFIC BIOLOGY **THE ORIGIN OF SPECIES** IS AMAZINGLY SIMPLE. IT'S WRITTEN IN SUCH STRAIGHTFORWARD ENGLISH THAT ANYONE WHO IS CAPABLE OF FOLLOWING A LOGICAL ARGUMENT CAN RECOGNIZE WHAT IT MEANS.

In fact **The Origin of Species** was a popular success. The first printing sold out on the day of publication. This alone distinguished it from most other great theories in the history of science. Isaac Newton's great work was, and still is, inaccessible to the general reader. The mathematical argument is so abstruse that it took many years of patient analysis before the **scientific** community fully understood its implications. The fact that Darwin's theory could be put so simply may have been one of the reasons Huxley asked himself why nobody had thought of it before.

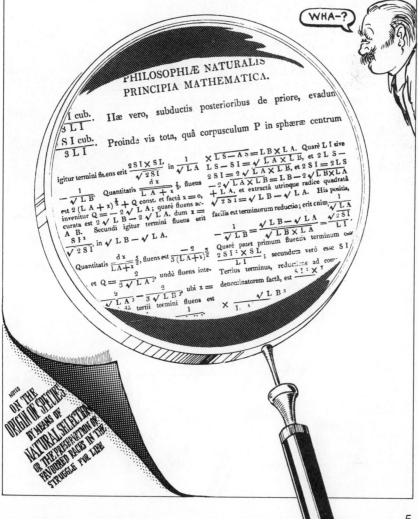

THIS IMPRESSION WAS REINFORCED BY DARWIN'S OWN PERSONALITY. HE SEEMED LITTLE MORE THAN AN AFFABLE AMATEUR, SOMEONE WHOSE FORMAL EDUCATION HAD BEEN A SERIES OF HUMILIATING DISASTERS.

NONE OF THIS DISCREDITS DARWIN'S ACHIEVEMENT. BUT IT DOES REVEAL SOMETHING RATHER PECULIAR ABOUT IT.

In fact, one reason why Darwin issued his book when he did, is that he was panicked into publishing by receiving through the post a summary of the theory which he'd been secretly nursing for twenty years.

By 1859, the scientific atmosphere was saturated with the possibility of evolution. It was only a matter of time before someone stumbled on the truth. Nevertheless the question remains: why hadn't it been recognized before?

One answer might be that the necessary facts weren't available until Darwin discovered them, and that he was lucky to find the missing pieces which allowed him to make sense of all the rest. But this isn't true either, for although Darwin made many important observations of his own, the facts which would have supported his theory were already known and had been widely discussed before. No one it seems had recognized their significance. Or not entirely.

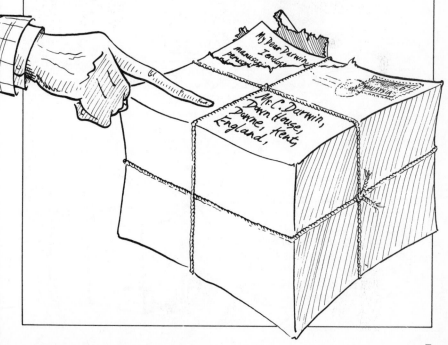

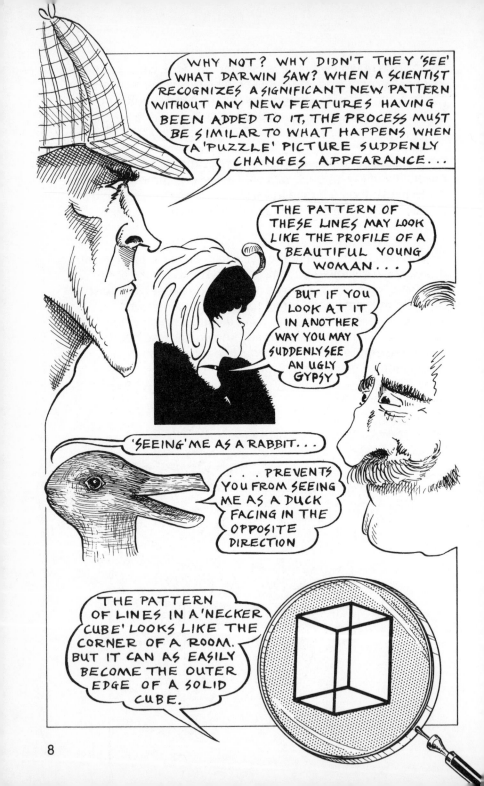

WHY NOT? WHY DIDN'T THEY 'SEE' WHAT DARWIN SAW? WHEN A SCIENTIST RECOGNIZES A SIGNIFICANT NEW PATTERN WITHOUT ANY NEW FEATURES HAVING BEEN ADDED TO IT, THE PROCESS MUST BE SIMILAR TO WHAT HAPPENS WHEN A 'PUZZLE' PICTURE SUDDENLY CHANGES APPEARANCE...

THE PATTERN OF THESE LINES MAY LOOK LIKE THE PROFILE OF A BEAUTIFUL YOUNG WOMAN...

BUT IF YOU LOOK AT IT IN ANOTHER WAY YOU MAY SUDDENLY SEE AN UGLY GYPSY

'SEEING' ME AS A RABBIT...

...PREVENTS YOU FROM SEEING ME AS A DUCK FACING IN THE OPPOSITE DIRECTION

THE PATTERN OF LINES IN A 'NECKER CUBE' LOOKS LIKE THE CORNER OF A ROOM. BUT IT CAN AS EASILY BECOME THE OUTER EDGE OF A SOLID CUBE.

The point is that a strong preconception about what a pattern **means**, what it represents, can stop you seeing it in any other way. Presumably this happened to Darwin's predecessors and some of his contemporaries as well. They failed to 'see' what Darwin 'saw', not because they were short of facts, but because they had reasons for 'seeing' the facts in a different way. They saw a duck and Darwin taught them to recognize a rabbit. Huxley's surprise was recognizing something that had been in front of his eyes all along.

The question is, what preconceptions led scientists to overlook the pattern that Darwin eventually saw? (Another question you will have to ask is whether Darwin really saw what he claimed to have seen, and whether his own position was quite as revolutionary as it has been said to be.)

There were several preconceptions which delayed the recognition of evolution in nature. And they arose from man's tendency to project the image of his own mind onto the world around him.
1. The biblical notion of special creation.
2. The Greek philosophical notion of Ideal Forms.

CREATIONISM

MOST SOCIETIES EXPLAIN THE ORIGIN OF THE LIVING WORLD AS AN ACT OF PROVIDENTIAL DESIGN. FOR WESTERN EUROPE, THIS DOCTRINE IS ENSHRINED IN THE BIBLE

According to the Book of Genesis God formed the world and stocked it with a wealth of clearly distinguishable living forms.
Christian theologians extracted several important dogmas from this myth.

For Christians, physical history was a short action-packed chapter bracketed between endless tracts of eternity. Such a short time-span ruled out the possibility of gradual change. Until scientists recognized that the age of the earth had to be reckoned in billions of years, evolutionary thought had no chance of gaining a foothold. This consideration will return to plague Darwin in his later years.

According to orthodox Christian thought, the appearance of the modern earth was the result of two factors:
1. The shape God had given it in the beginning.
2. The damage he inflicted on it when he punished man with the flood. The globe was a static ruin, and hadn't changed its basic structure since the deluge ploughed up the mountains and excavated the valleys. In a scene of such changeless monotony there was no need for living things to alter.

Once Adam had named all the plants and animals these inaugural forms bred true to type and never changed their identity.

WHEN GOD INUNDATED THE WORLD HE ORDERED NOAH TO SET ASIDE A REPRESENTATIVE PAIR OF EVERY LIVING TYPE, SO THAT AFTER THE FLOOD, THE WORLD WOULD BE REPOPULATED EXACTLY AS BEFORE.

For pious Christians it was an article of faith that the living world was an unaltered replica of the one which God had created at the outset. No species had been lost and none had been altered. Extinction was just as inconceivable as change.

For a long time this dogma led scientists to disregard the significance of fossils. The fact that these 'figured stones' happened to resemble shellfish etc. was often dismissed as an interesting coincidence, or as a sign that God had playfully decorated his rocks with ornamental replicas of living things.

ONCE THEIR ORGANIC CHARACTER WAS RECOGNIZED IT POSED AN AWKWARD PROBLEM. THE 17TH CENTURY NATURALIST, JOHN RAY ANNOUNCED THAT:

IT WOULD FOLLOW THAT MANY SPECIES OF SHELLFISH ARE LOST OUT OF THE WORLD WHICH PHILOSOPHERS HAVE HITHERTO BEEN UNWILLING TO ADMIT, ESTEEMING THE DESTRUCTION OF ANY ONE SPECIES A DISMEMBERING OF THE UNIVERSE AND RENDERING IT IMPERFECT; WHEREAS THEY THINK THE DIVINE PROVIDENCE IS ESPECIALLY CONCERNED TO PRESERVE AND SECURE THE WORK OF THE CREATION.

Instead of allowing the accidental extinction of a few imperfect types, it was less embarrassing to assume that God had deliberately destroyed all his living handiwork, only to recreate it all over again once man had been taught a lesson.

This idea had to be elaborated as geological discoveries revealed not one but **many** layers of extinct life. By the end of the 18th century, it was generally acknowledged that the rocks contained a whole record of a previous existence.

In order to avoid the blasphemous implication of continuous change, scientists introduced the theory of intermittent catastrophes. Instead of one flood it was now suggested that there had been many — Noah's being the last. After each cataclysm God had generously replenished the globe with a fresh stock of living things. It soon became apparent, however, that these successive creations were not simply repetitions of one another. Each fossil level showed a distinct advance on its predecessor. Invertebrates appeared in the lowest and oldest strata. Then fish began to figure. Reptiles and birds appeared later, then mammals and finally man.

THESE FINDINGS INTRODUCED THE IDEA OF **PROGRESSION!**

PROGRESSIONISM

God, it seemed, had staggered his creative efforts, allowing nature to develop in a series of separate stages. This **Progressionism** had nothing to do with evolution. There was no question of descent, no transition from one stage to the next. Each level represented a **unique** act of creation.

WRONG

RIGHT!

THE CONNECTION IS NOT THE CONSEQUENCE OF A DIRECT LINEAGE BETWEEN THE FAUNAS OF DIFFERENT AGES. THERE IS NOTHING LIKE PARENTAL DESCENT CONNECTING THEM. THE FISHES OF THE PALAEOZOIC AGE ARE IN NO RESPECT THE ANCESTORS OF THE REPTILES OF THE SECONDARY AGE, NOR DOES MAN DESCEND FROM THE MAMMALS WHICH PRECEDED HIM IN THE TERTIARY AGE. THE LINK BY WHICH THEY ARE CONNECTED IS OF A HIGHER IMMATERIAL NATURE; THEIR CONNECTION IS TO BE SOUGHT IN THE VIEW OF THE CREATOR HIMSELF, WHOSE AIM IN FORMING THE EARTH ..... WAS TO INTRODUCE MAN UPON ITS SURFACE.

LOUIS AGASSIZ

(19TH CENTURY PALAEONTOLOGIST)

Behind the dogmas of **Creationism** lay the notion of intelligent providential design. Although this is not explicitly mentioned in the Book of Genesis, it became the most forceful argument in favour of a Special Creation.

As biological research developed during the 18th century, scientists were more and more struck by the fitness and efficiency of living things. Fins, feathers, hearts, lungs and eyes were so admirably adapted to the functions they served, it seemed inconceivable they could have arisen spontaneously — let alone by chance. They **must** have been deliberately designed. Here at last was a **rational** argument in favour of God's existence. It was no longer necessary to rely on Biblical faith since the very facts of science bore witness to the activity of an intelligent designer.

This Natural Theology gave traditional Christianity a new lease of life. When Darwin was growing up, the argument from design was a most powerful objection to evolutionary thought. Nature was a living record of God's benevolent foresight.

SUPPOSE ONE HAD NEVER SEEN A WATCH BEFORE

THE MOST FAMOUS EXPRESSION OF THIS ARGUMENT WAS BISHOP PALEY'S **EVIDENCE OF CHRISTIANITY**

<u>NOW</u> APPLY THIS PRINCIPLE TO THE **EYE**! THE TRANSPARENCY OF THE CORNEA, THE PRECISION OF THE LENS, AND THE ADJUSTABILITY OF THE PUPIL, ALL CO-OPERATE TO SERVE VISION. THE MARKS OF DESIGN ARE TOO STRONG TO BE GOTTEN OVER. DESIGN MUST HAVE A DESIGNER. THAT DESIGNER MUST BE A PERSON . . .

Darwin knew Paley's book by heart, and confessed that in his youth he had been enchanted by its unarguable logic. Even Huxley assumed that intelligent creation was the most plausible explanation for the beautiful efficiency of nature.

In the early years of the 19th century, the argument from design spearheaded the attack on evolutionary thought.

In England the religious dogmas of **Creationism** played an especially important part in delaying evolutionary thought. This was partly because the Anglican church was built-in to the political structure of Great Britain, and any threat to Christian orthodoxy implied an even greater threat to social stability.

Although the doctrine of **Creationism** played an important part in continental thought, the **Philosophical Idealism of Plato** was just as important, if not more so. This notion is also known as **Essentialism**.

According to Plato, the physical world was a mirage from which little reliable information could be gained. The only things which really existed were changeless **Ideas** or **Forms**; and the objects which existed in the physical world were distorted changeable shadows of these permanent unalterable essences.

This meant that change and variation were mere illusions, and **genuine** reality consisted of fixed types, permanently distinguished from one another.

PHYSICAL TABLES MIGHT DIFFER FROM ONE ANOTHER, BUT THE *ESSENTIAL TABLE* - THE *IDEAL* GENUINE TABLE - THE DISTINCT TYPE WHICH LIES BENEATH ALL THESE DIFFERENCES IS FIXED FOREVER. A PERMANENT STEREOTYPE WHICH OUTLASTS CHANGE AND TRANSCENDS VARIATION.

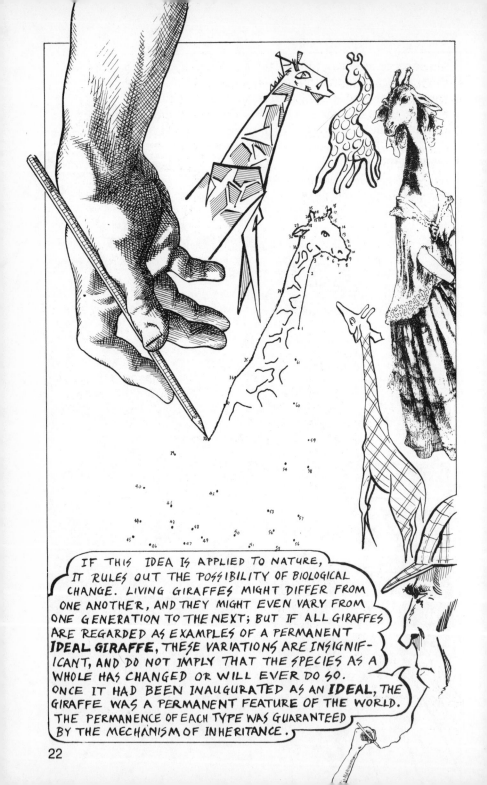

IF THIS IDEA IS APPLIED TO NATURE,
IT RULES OUT THE POSSIBILITY OF BIOLOGICAL
CHANGE. LIVING GIRAFFES MIGHT DIFFER FROM
ONE ANOTHER, AND THEY MIGHT EVEN VARY FROM
ONE GENERATION TO THE NEXT; BUT IF ALL GIRAFFES
ARE REGARDED AS EXAMPLES OF A PERMANENT
IDEAL GIRAFFE, THESE VARIATIONS ARE INSIGNIF-
ICANT, AND DO NOT IMPLY THAT THE SPECIES AS A
WHOLE HAS CHANGED OR WILL EVER DO SO.
ONCE IT HAD BEEN INAUGURATED AS AN **IDEAL**, THE
GIRAFFE WAS A PERMANENT FEATURE OF THE WORLD.
THE PERMANENCE OF EACH TYPE WAS GUARANTEED
BY THE MECHANISM OF INHERITANCE.

Since antiquity there had been two conflicting theories about the way in which biological form is maintained from one generation to the next.

1. According to **Aristotle** and his followers, the development of the foetus is the fulfilment of an idea. As if the fertilized egg contains a spiritual power working towards a predetermined end. (Rather like a sculptor forming a statue from a block of featureless marble.)

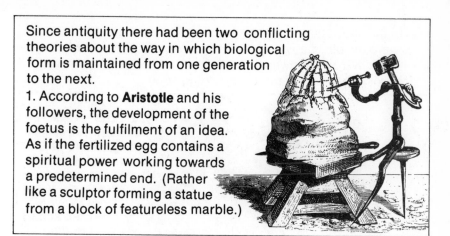

WHEN **WILLIAM HARVEY** DEVELOPED THIS IDEA IN THE 17TH CENTURY, HE TURNED ARISTOTLE ON HIS HEAD...

23

2. In the late 17th century, biologists such as **Malpighi** put forward the alternative theory of **Preformation**, according to which, development was the unfolding and enlargement of a pre-existing model of the forthcoming adult.

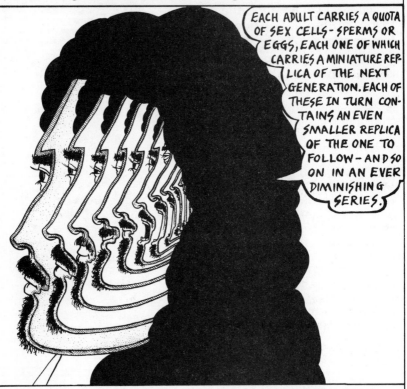

EACH ADULT CARRIES A QUOTA OF SEX CELLS - SPERMS OR EGGS, EACH ONE OF WHICH CARRIES A MINIATURE REPLICA OF THE NEXT GENERATION. EACH OF THESE IN TURN CONTAINS AN EVEN SMALLER REPLICA OF THE ONE TO FOLLOW - AND SO ON IN AN EVER DIMINISHING SERIES.

For each living type, God or Providence had made a nest of 'Russian dolls', and it was simply a question of unpacking them one after another. Reproduction automatically preserved the characteristics of the inaugural type, and change was pre-empted from the outset. This theory of so-called **Emboitement** became very popular in the 18th century; and since it left no room for change, it represented an insuperable block to evolutionary thought.

In fact, the mechanism of inheritance remained a major difficulty till the end of the 19th century. Until scientists properly understood how biological form was **maintained** from one generation to the next, it was impossible to explain how it could be **modified**.

Plato's notion of **Forms** and **Ideas** was associated with the equally famous doctrine of the **Great Chain of Being**.

According to Aristotle, nature was not simply a list of ideal types, but an orderly ladder.

This ladder was grounded in inanimate matter, and rose step by step towards immaterial spirit. Suspended between were the various ranks of living things. First simple plants, and then primitive animals. Next came fish, then reptiles, followed by birds and mammals.

Half way up the flight of stairs stood man — half body and half spirit. Above him came the various orders of disembodied angels, and above all was God himself. This arrangement provided the 18th century with a monumentally static picture of nature.

This picture had a strong appeal for all those with a vested interest in maintaining the traditional structure of human society. The existence of a great chain of being explained and justified the inequalities of man, and vindicated a society in which everyone knew his place and no one had pretensions to rise.

It is not surprising that the recognition of change in nature coincided with the revolutionary transformation of society.

By the end of the 18th century the ground was beginning to shift under most of the dogmas we've just listed. Darwin had not overturned them single-handed. By the time he published **The Origin of Species** in 1859, the scientific world was ready to accept what he said. To some extent this was the result of what had been happening in the other sciences — in physics, in astronomy and especially in geology.

Throughout the Christian Middle Ages, the Universe was regarded as a closed system, centred on man and directed by God.

From the 19th century onwards this picture began to undergo a slow but irreversible transformation. The earth was removed from the centre of things and set moving amongst the planets. The closed

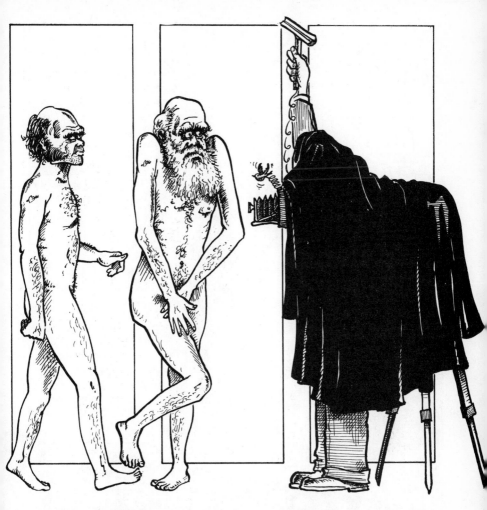

world gradually gave way to an infinite universe.

Physical events were governed by natural laws, and although God was still recognized as the author of these statutes, his personal intervention was no longer required in order to explain how things were made.

The emphasis slowly shifted from the supernatural to the natural. From the miraculous to the mundane. And although the cosmos was still regarded as something which had been created, it was also seen as a developing process subject to scientific laws.

It was only a matter of time before this attitude influenced the study of the Earth.

UNIFORMITARIANISM

INSTEAD OF SEEING THE GLOBE AS A RUINED MONUMENT, DEFACED BY PREHISTORIC CATACLYSMS, 18th CENTURY SCIENTISTS BEGAN TO RECOGNISE THAT IT HAD UNDERGONE CONTINUOUS PHYSICAL CHANGE. THE NATURAL FORCES NOW AT WORK WERE THE ONES WHICH HAD ALWAYS BEEN SHAPING ITS PHYSICAL FEATURES.

FOR THE SCOTTISH GEOLOGIST **JAMES HUTTON**, THE TERRESTRIAL GLOBE WAS AND ALWAYS HAD BEEN THE PROVINCE OF TERRESTRIAL PROCESSES. WIND, RAIN & FROST. EROSION, SUBSIDENCE AND SEDIMENTATION. AND, ABOVE ALL, THE TITANIC AND UNCEASING COOKERY OF VOLCANIC HEAT.

In his theory of the earth, published in 1788, Hutton introduced the doctrine of **Uniformitarianism**.

This theory overturned the **Catastrophic** history of the world, changing it from a series of separate tableaux into a slow-motion movie.

Hutton's work was largely overlooked by his immediate contemporaries. But it was taken up, developed and popularised, by the great 19th century geologist...**Charles Lyell**.

By mobilizing the history of the globe, Lyell set the stage for the possibility of continuous biological change. Although Lyell was reluctant to recognise the transformation of species, his theory of geological change made biological evolution inevitable.

Huxley later wrote "I cannot but believe that Lyell was for others, as for me, the chief agent in smoothing the road for Darwin".

AND SO THE CASE COMES TO TRIAL...

Facts In Favour
Of Evolution Before Darwin

Exhibit A
The sequence of Fossil Types

Human life is so short and the span of biological time so long. it is impossible to observe evolution as it happens.

Nevertheless, by 1830 there was plenty of circumstantial evidence.

CALL ADAM SEDGWICK!

AS A GEOLOGIST, I RECOGNISE THAT THERE WAS A GRADUAL ASCENT TOWARDS A HIGHER TYPE OF BEING. BUT AS A PIOUS CHRISTIAN I DO NOT REGARD THIS AS EVIDENCE OF CONTINUOUS TRANSFORMATION.

Anyway, the large gaps in the fossil record reinforced the impression of a series of separate creations, separated by comprehensive miraculous catastrophes. Nevertheless, the geological progress of fossil types would later become an important part of evolutionary theory. As geology improved, the gaps between one era and the next became ever smaller so that the notion of **continuous** transformation became more convincing.

In any case, there was already convincing evidence that the cataclysms were not as complete as the theologians supposed, and that some types persisted unchanged.

Exhibit B
The Existence of Rudimentary Organs

By the end of the 18th century, biologists knew that living animals contained small remnants of functionless organs. Flightless insects, for instance, are often equipped with tiny functionless wings. Certain snakes retain aborted fragments of useless limbs. Such facts made nonsense of the argument from design.

I PUT IT TO THE WITNESS THAT GOD HAS RETAINED SUCH STRUCTURES IN ORDER TO PRESERVE SYMMETRY.

SILENCE IN COURT

But Darwin recognised they could be explained much better on the assumption that such creatures had descended from ancestors equipped with fully developed organs, and had gradually lost them as they adapted to new ways of living.

Darwin was struck by the fact "That the hand of a man formed for grasping, that of a mole for digging, the leg of the horse, the paddle of the porpoise, and the wing of the bat, should all be constructed on the same pattern, and should include the same bones in the same relative positions". For the **Essentialists** this was evidence of a uniform plan in the mind of the creator. A manufacturer's idiom. Darwin did not accept this explanation. He assumed that the various creatures had descended from a common ancestor and the primitive stereotype had been continuously modified as they became adapted to different ways of living.

18th century comparative anatomists noted the fact that as creatures developed, they went through stages which resembled the adult forms of more primitive types. In the early stages, the human foetus, for example, has gill slits which are strikingly similar to those of the fish. There are phases in their development in which it is almost impossible to distinguish between the embryos of reptiles, birds and mammals. Once again this could be interpreted as evidence of a designer's scheme. But Darwin recognised it as one more fact in favour of common descent.

In any case, the embryologists of the early 19th century over-simplified their account of what was called **Recapitulation**. They insisted that each embryo had to **repeat** the adult stages of its biological predecessors. In the process of becoming a man, a human foetus does not **have** to become a cod first, next a lizard, and then a monkey. It passes instead through a strictly human sequence of development in the course of which it resembles, without actually reproducing, the comparable stages of its more primitive relatives. In **The Origin of Species** Darwin emphasized the crucial importance of embryological evidence.

The facts of Animal & Plant Breeding

AGRICULTURE & ANIMAL HUSBANDRY SHOULD HAVE PROVIDED OVERWHELMING EVIDENCE AGAINST THE PREVAILING NOTION OF THE RIGID STABILITY OF LIVING TYPES.

Farmers and breeders were well aware that livestock of the same species display an extraordinary variety of forms, and that many of these differences are inherited from one generation to the next. Selective breeding could give rise to new strains. Once established, these become relatively permanent. For those obstinately dedicated to the notion of permanent essences or types, such transformations were negligible variations.

Darwin regarded them as an experimental model of what was happening all the time in nature. For him, variation and difference was the genuine reality, and stability and permanence was an illusion.

36

The Struggle For Existence

ERASMUS

BUFFON

It was known, long before Darwin, that animals multiplied much faster than the available food supply. This inevitably led to a lethal competition for existence. The French naturalist **Comte G.L.L. de Buffon** recognised this, and so did Darwin's grandfather **Erasmus**. But Charles Darwin was the first scientist to draw the comparison between the selection exerted by nature and the choice that was exercised by animal breeders.

Exhibit 6
The Evidence of New Explorations

The biblical account of Creation was seriously disturbed when explorers of the 16th and 17th centuries began to discover animals not mentioned in the Book of Genesis. The New World was stocked with species similar but not identical to those already familiar in the old. This made it necessary to assume God had undertaken subsidiary acts of creation for the purpose of populating America and Australia.

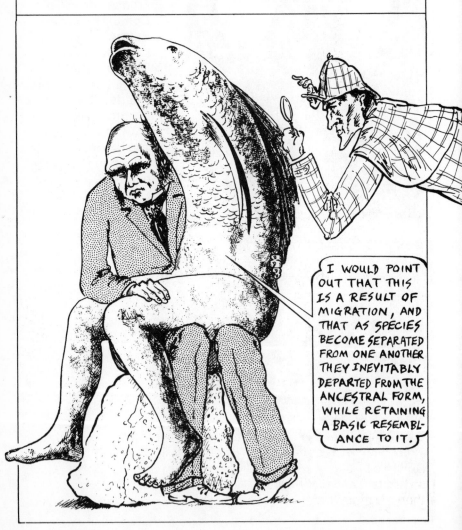

I WOULD POINT OUT THAT THIS IS A RESULT OF MIGRATION, AND THAT AS SPECIES BECOME SEPARATED FROM ONE ANOTHER THEY INEVITABLY DEPARTED FROM THE ANCESTRAL FORM, WHILE RETAINING A BASIC RESEMBLANCE TO IT.

These facts were separately recognised long before Darwin. In spite of the prejudice in favour of **creationism, essentialism,** and **providential design,** the evolutionary implications were so strong that there had been several attempts to suggest the continuous transformation of nature.

As early as 1749, the French naturalist Buffon conceded that the age of the earth had been seriously underestimated; that living things had probably undergone considerable alteration.

Buffon did not give a coherent account of this change. And although he separately identified much of the evidence which Darwin later regarded as crucial, he failed to realise the solution which later dazzled Huxley by its obviousness.

Buffon's theory of evolution — he called it "degradation" — was so hesitant and half-hearted that it had much less influence than the more forceful fiction of his famous colleague Lamarck.

Like his 18th century colleagues, **J.B.A.P. de Monet Lamarck** was devoted to the traditional doctrine of the Great Chain of Being. For him, nature was a graded series of natural types, arranged in order: from the simplest and most microscopic, to the largest and most complicated. The difference was that Lamarck regarded this as an escalator rather than a stairway.

From the moment when God had first created it, nature was endlessly on the move. All creatures were caught up in the struggle to become as complicated as men. In order to fill the emptying lower steps of the escalator, Lamarck found it necessary to suggest an endless process of spontaneous generation. In order to replenish the scale of being, inanimate matter had to form itself into simple creatures which then stepped on to the bottom of the escalator and filled the gap left by those rising towards the top.

Lamarck suggested that this onward and upward progress was directed by two natural forces.

1. **The inherent drive towards increasing complexity.**
Living matter was as if imbued with a natural ambition to be bigger and better, so that each creature was irresistibly drawn towards a higher stage of development.

2. The shaping power of the environment

According to Lamarck, the natural habits of a creature would inevitably lead to a modification of its anatomical structure. By wading in shallow water a bird would stretch its legs in order to keep its body above the surface, and automatically acquire longer limbs. Once this addition was acquired it would be handed on to the next generation, and so on. Conversely, the disuse of a structure would automatically lead to its shrinkage, and this too would be inherited by the successors.

As it turned out, Lamarck's theory contained fewer truths than Buffon's; but its systematic persuasiveness was so strong that it was the most influential of all evolutionary theories until Darwin. It was almost certainly the inspiration for Erasmus Darwin's theory of biological transformation, and probably responsible for the most famous of all evolutionary theories in the mid-19th century.

In 1844 the respectable world was outraged by the publication of an anonymous book entitled **The Vestiges of the Natural History of the Creation**.

This work, which suggested that the succession of fossil types was evidence of an unceasing transformation of what God had created at the beginning of time, caused a major scandal throughout western Europe. In drawing-rooms and at dinner-parties there was wide speculation as to the identity of its blasphemous author.

The uproar and scandal which Chambers' work created was one reason why Darwin postponed publication of his own theory. As early as 1838, he had already formulated the essential outlines of what later became **The Origin of Species.** Darwin confessed to one of his friends that he was already entertaining the idea of the transformation of species.

IT'S LIKE CONFESSING TO A MURDER...

By the time Darwin overcame his scruples in 1859, the scientific world was thoroughly familiar with the issue of evolution. Again, this is why Huxley rebuked himself for not thinking of it before.

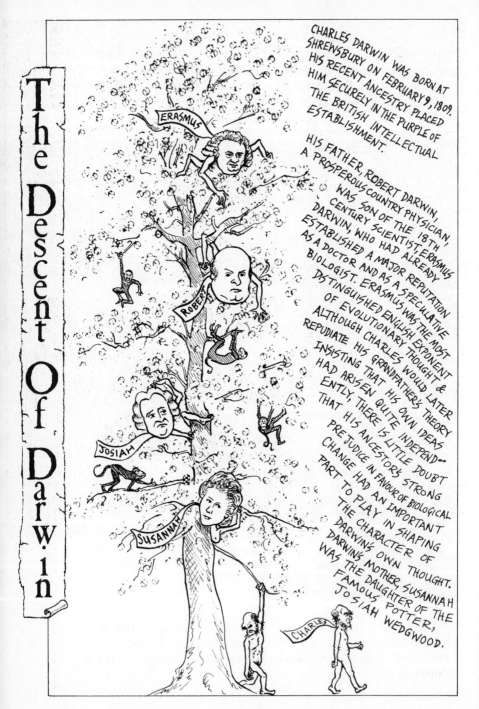

The Descent Of Darwin

ERASMUS

ROBERT

JOSIAH

SUSANNAH

CHARLES

CHARLES DARWIN WAS BORN AT SHREWSBURY ON FEBRUARY 9, 1809. HIS RECENT ANCESTRY PLACED HIM SECURELY IN THE PURPLE OF THE BRITISH INTELLECTUAL ESTABLISHMENT.

HIS FATHER, ROBERT DARWIN, A PROSPEROUS COUNTRY PHYSICIAN, WAS SON OF THE 18TH CENTURY SCIENTIST, ERASMUS DARWIN, WHO HAD ALREADY ESTABLISHED A MAJOR REPUTATION AS A DOCTOR AND AS A SPECULATIVE BIOLOGIST. ERASMUS WAS THE MOST DISTINGUISHED ENGLISH EXPONENT OF EVOLUTIONARY THOUGHT & ALTHOUGH CHARLES WOULD LATER REPUDIATE HIS GRANDFATHER'S THEORY INSISTING THAT HIS OWN IDEAS HAD ARISEN QUITE INDEPEND-- ENTLY, THERE IS LITTLE DOUBT THAT HIS ANCESTOR'S STRONG PREJUDICE IN FAVOUR OF BIOLOGICAL CHANGE HAD AN IMPORTANT PART TO PLAY IN SHAPING THE CHARACTER OF DARWIN'S OWN THOUGHT. DARWIN'S MOTHER, SUSANNAH WAS THE DAUGHTER OF THE FAMOUS POTTER, JOSIAH WEDGWOOD.

The Wedgwood connection had been established in the previous generation, when Erasmus struck up a long-lasting friendship with the Staffordshire potter Josiah Wedgwood. Both men belonged to the Lunar Society of Birmingham — an informal club whose members, consisting of Midland scientists and manufacturers, met once a month on the occasion of the new moon to discuss technology and other subjects of shared interest.

The society included men such as **Matthew Boulton,** the Birmingham engineer, his partner **James Watt** who invented the separate condenser steam-engine, and many other distinguished provincial intellectuals. They discussed the chemistry of clays and glazes, surveying, geology, and the recently developed science of climate and weather. They projected plans for new canals, and devices for harnessing the power of wind and steam. The Lunar Society was the intellectual seedbed of the industrial revolution. The acceptable face of Capitalism.

Inadvertently, these men were responsible for nudging English thought towards the characteristic secularism of the twentieth century. The profitable results of treating nature as a manageable process led them to disregard its theological significance, and focus instead on the intelligible laws which governed its behaviour.

The thought that money might be made out of something, is apt to concentrate the mind wonderfully. If profit can be increased by setting aside any thought of God's intentions, businessmen are only too eager to take up the option. The pursuit of science usually leads to the achievement of prosperity; and, for a while, the habit of inquisitive Godlessness becomes a way of life.

For that reason, the dogmas of Christianity were beginning to lose their grip on the members of the Lunar Society. Although few of them would have admitted to out-and-out atheism, they no longer looked to God as an explanation for everything that happened in the natural world.

The point is, scientific curiosity is not a native human talent. It has to be shaped and directed by social situations; institutional arrangements and vested interests, which give certain inquiries their characteristic verve and momentum.

Historians have long been familiar with the relationship between religion and the rise of capitalism. But scientists have often overlooked the economic antecedents of their own profession, preferring to regard it as the pure and unadulterated expression of the need for objective inquiry.

With a family background such as his, Charles Darwin's professional future should have been guaranteed from the outset. But his early career was a bitter disappointment to his father.

Young Charles was sent to school at Shrewsbury in 1818. His career was spectacularly undistinguished. He was taught little and learned less.

Nevertheless, he showed an early interest in collecting minerals, insects, and birds' eggs. Darwin senior regarded these pursuits as a self-indulgent waste of time.

IN THE EFFORT TO GIVE HIM A RESPECTABLE CAREER, DARWIN'S FATHER TOOK HIM OUT OF SHREWSBURY SCHOOL, & IN 1825 SENT HIM TO EDINBURGH UNIVERSITY TO STUDY MEDICINE.

HUME   SMITH   STEWART

From the middle of the 18th century, Edinburgh had been one of the most distinguished intellectual cities in Europe. This "Athens of the North" was the centre of the Scottish Enlightenment. Sober, serious and patrician. Philosophers such as **Hume, Adam Smith** and **Dugald Stewart;** chemists, theologians and social scientists. Medicine flourished there as the queen of the human sciences, benefiting from a long established association with the great Netherlands University of Leyden. During the Napoleonic war, when medical students were prevented from going to Leyden, Edinburgh became the Mecca for anyone with serious medical ambitions.

Young Darwin, however, had no such ambition, and found the medical curriculum a dreary ordeal. His kind heart and tender feelings were outraged by the nauseating sights and sounds of an amputation without anaesthetic. He found most of the other lectures incredibly dull, leaving him with a memory of "cold, breakfastless hours, listening to discourses on the properties of rhubarb".

In formal terms, the sixteen year old medical student wasted as much time at Edinburgh as he already had in Shrewsbury. Nevertheless, he was laying the foundations of his future achievement. He read widely, continued making his collections, and pursued the study of natural history. He went on dredging expeditions in the Firth of Forth, and dissected many of the marine specimens which he found.

He made friends with a black taxidermist who taught him how to skin and stuff birds, a skill which would stand him in good stead during his voyage round the world. Darwin's affable readiness to form a professional relationship with someone then regarded as a member of an "inferior race", distinguished him from some of his more orthodox colleagues. He probably inherited his easy-going tolerance from his grandfather Erasmus, an eager exponent of the abolition of slavery. For Darwin, the brotherhood of man would eventually be seen as part and parcel of the Fraternity of Life.

Darwin also made friends with the Edinburgh zoologist, **Robert Grant,** who startled the young medical student whilst on a walk by giving a favourable account of Lamarck's theory of evolution. This was probably the young Darwin's first introduction to a thoroughgoing theory of biological transformation.

He also became a member of the Plinian Society, an academic club in which scientific papers of natural history were read.

At one of these meetings, Darwin first came face-to-face with the dangers of expressing blasphemous opinions in science. One of the members delivered a paper expressing Materialist views of the nature of life. Darwin was startled to discover all records of this were later struck out of the Society's Minutes. This experience may have been one reason why Darwin put off publication of his own theory for nearly twenty years.

During the 1820's, young Darwin was still a Christian, although not a zealous enthusiast. He found no difficulty in subscribing to the Thirty Nine Articles, and accepted the prospect of becoming a country clergyman.

At the end of 1827 he entered Christ's College Cambridge. He was dismayed to discover that he had already forgotten what little Greek he knew.

However, he scraped through his entrance exam, and enrolled at the University. He immediately fell into his old ways, and hobnobbed with the sporting gentry of his college. Like Thackeray's Pendennis he shot, hunted and gambled his days away, and confessed that when the shooting season started, nervous excitement made his hands shake so much that he could scarcely load his gun.

His interest in natural history was unabated and he struck up further scientific friendships which were to influence the course of his career. He was more or less adopted by the clergyman botanist, **John Stevens Henslow,** who took him on long plant-collecting expeditions.

Unlike Robert Grant, however, Henslow
was an obstinate upholder of Creationism, and refused to accept the possibility of transformation of species. Another friend was the geologist **Adam Sedgwick** who awakened Darwin's interest in the formation of the earth.

Meanwhile, two books exerted an even more important influence on Darwin's thought. **Alexander Humboldt's Personal Narrative** — an amazingly popular scientific travelogue which infected Darwin with irresistible wanderlust. A more subtle influence was **John Herschel's Introduction to the Study of Natural Philosophy** which gave Darwin his first inkling of rigorous scientific thought.

FOR THE INTELLECTUALS OF THE 19TH CENTURY, THE ASTRONOMER HERSCHEL BECAME THE PARAGON OF SCIENTIFIC PERFECTION. ANYONE TRYING TO BE A SCIENTIST WAS ADVISED TO BE AS MUCH LIKE HERSCHEL AS POSSIBLE. FROM THIS BOOK DARWIN LEARNT THE DIFFICULT TASK OF BRINGING TOGETHER CONJECTURE AND FACTS. IT TAUGHT HIM THE NEED TO RECONCILE CAUTION WITH COURAGE.

During a University vacation in 1831, Sedgwick took Darwin on a geological expedition to North Wales, and thereby confirmed a lifelong interest in the arrangement of layers and strata.

SEDGWICK

Less than a year later, with the publication of the first volume of Lyell's **Principles of Geology,** Darwin was converted from his earlier Catastrophism to a thoroughgoing Uniformitarianism. From now on, he too would see the earth as a self-servicing machine, gradually transforming its appearance under the influence of forces which could be seen acting at this very moment. Another name for this was **Actualism**.

On his return in August, Darwin found a letter from his friend **Henslow** inviting him to take up a post as ship's naturalist on one of His Majesty's surveying vessels.

2.

I have stated that I consider you to be the just qualified person I know of who is likely to undertake such a situation. I state this not in the supposition of your being a *finished* naturalist, but as amply qualified for collecting, observing and noting anything worthy to be noted in Natural History...

Captain Fitzroy wants a man (I understand) more as a companion than a mere collector, and would not take anyone, however good a naturalist who was not recommended to him likewise as a gentleman...

Don't put any doubts or fears about your disqualifications, for I assure you I think you are the very man they are in search of.

Darwin's father was enraged by this invitation since it seemed to offer yet another postponement to his son's career. But his uncle Josiah overcame the paternal opposition.

Chart show __ oogy characters reveal'd through animal/human physiognomy

On the 5th September, Darwin was interviewed by Captain FitzRoy of HMS Beagle. At this point, the whole project very nearly came to grief. FitzRoy, a devotee of the fashionable science of Physiognomy, took exception to the shape of Darwin's nose, thinking that it betrayed signs of laziness and hesitancy. For some reason, FitzRoy overcame his scruples and Darwin was signed on.

Departure was delayed for several weeks. During this time Darwin was afflicted with nervous headaches.

These two months at Plymouth were the most miserable which I ever spent, though I exerted myself in various ways. I was out of spirits at the thought of leaving all my family and friends for so long a time, and the weather seemed to me inexpressibly gloomy. I was also troubled with palpitations about the heart, & like many a young ignorant man, specially one with a smattering of medical Knowledge, was convinced that I had heart disease. I did not consult any doctor as I fully expected to hear the ver-dict that I was not fit for the voyage, as I was resolved to go at all hazards

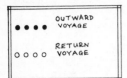

HMS Beagle was a Royal Navy 10 gun
sloop-brig. 235 tons, 90 foot long
and 24 foot in the beam.

On the 10th of December everything was ready, and the ship
set sail. The journey was to last longer than Darwin expected,
and he did not set foot in England for another five years.

Detailed accounts of this historic journey have been well
described elsewhere, above all in Darwin's own journal.

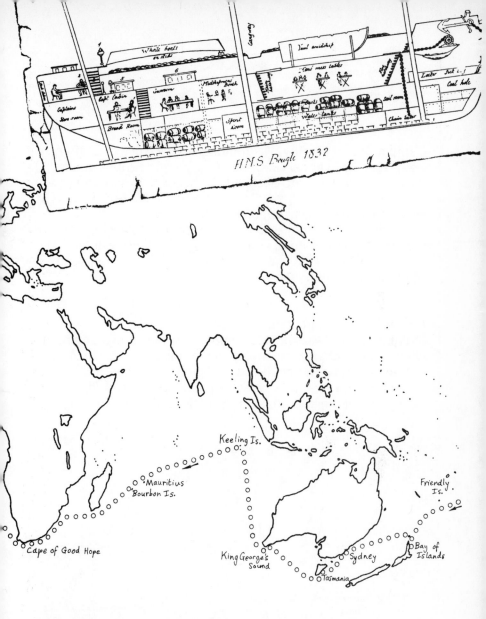

This map summarizes the itinerary and shows how the Beagle
slowly worked her way around the world, surveying the coastal
waters, charting the depths, and indicating the great ocean
currents. At certain points, Darwin left the ship to make long
overland excursions in South America, rejoining the vessel
after long expeditions into the mountains and windswept
pampas grasslands.

Captain Robert FitzRoy RN, grandson of the Duke of Grafton, was a zealous Evangelical Christian. By some curious quirk of fortune, the young naturalist had berthed with a man who was opposed to everything that Darwin stood for. FitzRoy was an avowed Creationist; an upholder of the political and social establishment; and unlike Darwin, he regarded slavery as an expression of the natural order of things. Locked together in the cramped tiny ship, the two men represented the opposite poles of 19th century thought.

One writer has characterised these personalities as **Mutaphobic** and **Mutaphiliac** respectively: one temperament which abhors change and upholds the standing order of things — tradition, royalty, obedience, and piety; the other temperament which celebrates alteration, progress and improvement. An unpromising start for a shipboard romance.

Not that Darwin was a disbeliever. He was still a Christian when the Beagle set sail, and in all probability still a Creationist. His social opinions, however, soon brought him into conflict with Captain FitzRoy. There were several embarrassing rows on the subject of slavery.

THE WEDGWOOD ANTI-SLAVERY MEDALLION

Darwin was also horrified by the inhuman rigours of naval discipline.

I THOUGHT I TOLD YOU TO WASH THIS BLOODY FLOOR

Close confinement taught him to curb his tongue. Darwin had an almost pathological dislike for heated controversy. This dislike for stirring up trouble would be yet another reason for delaying publication of his controversial theory.

He contented himself instead with an almost super-human industriousness.

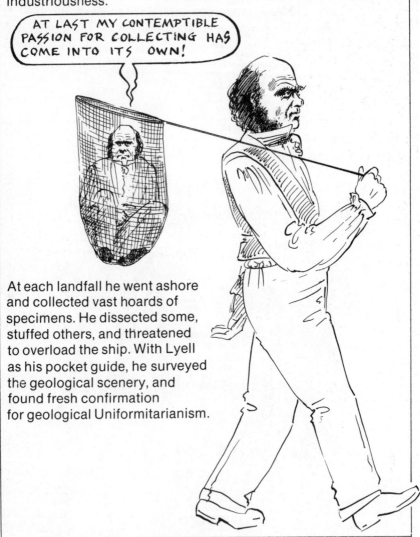

At each landfall he went ashore and collected vast hoards of specimens. He dissected some, stuffed others, and threatened to overload the ship. With Lyell as his pocket guide, he surveyed the geological scenery, and found fresh confirmation for geological Uniformitarianism.

For the young naturalist it was a miraculous rebirth. For years he was freed from the nagging restraints of his over-ambitious father, and from the stuffy decorum of early Victorian England. His health was restored and he experienced a vigorous energy which he would never enjoy again.

The moral and spiritual experience of the voyage was the most important contribution to Darwin's achievement. It gave him the freedom to put his thoughts in order, and to see things in their true perspective. Like Alice, whose adventures through the looking-glass enabled her to see things the right way up only after she had seen things upside-down, Darwin had to make a journey round the world in order to recognise what had been in front of his nose all the time. Nevertheless, certain crucial facts were brought to his attention; and although these (or facts very like them) were already available before he set sail, his direct experience of them played an essential part in crystallizing the great theory.

During the voyage however, there is little evidence to show that Darwin was **consciously** thinking about the mutability of species. And although he filled notebook after notebook with observations on biology and natural history, he did not visualize this material as an argument in favour of evolution.

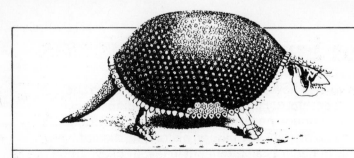

His geological interests took precedence over everything else. As the journey progressed, the influence of Lyell's great book gradually but irreversibly converted him to a Uniformitarian view.

On the 26th of October 1832, Darwin received the second volume of Lyell's textbook in which the geologist introduced and indignantly criticised Lamarck's theory of the transmutation of species — the same theory which Robert Grant had mentioned on one of those Edinburgh walks. Presumably these arguments sank into Darwin's subconscious. He was probably convinced by Lyell's rejection of the theory. But, at some level of Darwin's imagination, the conflict between Lyell's Uniformitarian geology and his Creationist biology must have struck him as inconsistent.

For, at a later date, when Darwin came to survey and summarize the biological observations he had made on the voyage, he recalled three groups of facts which made it difficult to accept the Immutability of Species.

1. The Succession of Types

I AM STRUCK BY THE STARTLING RESEMBLANCE BETWEEN THE FOSSILS OF CERTAIN EXTINCT ARMADILLOS AND THE SKELETONS OF LIVING SPECIES. ADMITTEDLY, THE EXTINCT FORMS WERE MUCH LARGER, BUT THEIR FORMAL RESEMBLANCE IS TOO STRIKING TO BE ACCIDENTAL!

DARWIN WOULD **LATER** SEE THIS VERTICAL SUCCESSION AS EVIDENCE OF CONTINUOUS DESCENT WITH MODIFICATION.

2. Representative Types

The resemblance between **historical** successors was mirrored by a corresponding similarity between **geographical** neighbours. Travelling across the South American pampas, Darwin noticed certain forms of ostrich were gradually replaced by distinct, but nevertheless similar types. Each area was populated by its own distinct representative form. Darwin later saw this not as the result of separate creations, but as the inevitable consequence of geographical separation. Migrating in opposite directions, the primitive ancestors of these two types had become so widely separated from one another that they could no longer freely interbreed.

WE HAVE INEVITABLY DIVERGED, DEVELOPING OUR RESPECTIVE DIFFERENCES TO THE POINT WHERE WE CAN NO LONGER INTERBREED.

EVEN IF WE WERE ALLOWED TO DO SO.

3. The Evidence of Ocean Islands

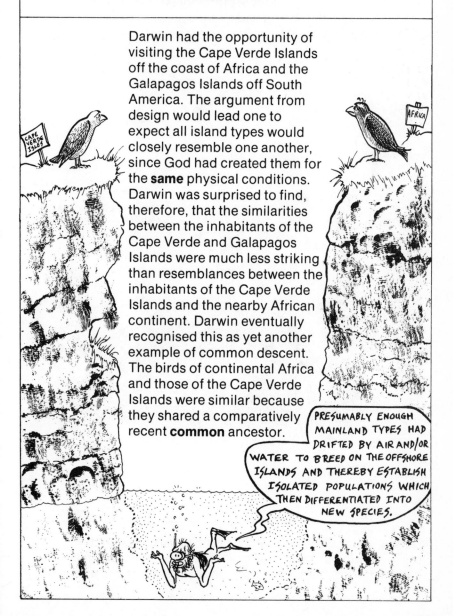

Darwin had the opportunity of visiting the Cape Verde Islands off the coast of Africa and the Galapagos Islands off South America. The argument from design would lead one to expect all island types would closely resemble one another, since God had created them for the **same** physical conditions. Darwin was surprised to find, therefore, that the similarities between the inhabitants of the Cape Verde and Galapagos Islands were much less striking than resemblances between the inhabitants of the Cape Verde Islands and the nearby African continent. Darwin eventually recognised this as yet another example of common descent. The birds of continental Africa and those of the Cape Verde Islands were similar because they shared a comparatively recent **common** ancestor.

PRESUMABLY ENOUGH MAINLAND TYPES HAD DRIFTED BY AIR AND/OR WATER TO BREED ON THE OFFSHORE ISLANDS AND THEREBY ESTABLISH ISOLATED POPULATIONS WHICH THEN DIFFERENTIATED INTO NEW SPECIES.

CAPE VERDE ISLES

AFRICA

Darwin found vivid examples of this process amongst the little islands of the Galapagos, desolate volcanic outcrops off the coast of South America. He noticed each one had its own distinct population of animals and birds. In spite of the fact that the ecological conditions were more or less identical from island to island, the lizards and finches on each were unmistakably **different** from those on the next.

Darwin would later see that the fauna on islands were the topmost twigs of a common branch: that oceanic separation had left the populations to vary **independently** of one another.

Darwin had seen and recorded all these facts without recognizing the picture they represented. Hindsight revealed the pattern – events recollected in the tranquility of homecoming. Only on the last leg of the journey, when Darwin began to put his notes in order, did he recognize the first stirrings of evolutionary thought.

In his great book **The Road to Xanadu** John Livingston Lowes discusses the origins of Coleridge's **Ancient Mariner**. He shows how the facts and images Coleridge obtained from ceaseless reading eventually returned to be incorporated in one of the greatest poems of the English language. Lowes points out that this material would have been useless, unless it had been **forgotten** first. It had to be plunged into the transforming depths of Coleridge's unconscious imagination before it could be retrieved and reordered.

Darwin was his own ancient mariner. Like Coleridge, he was unable to appreciate what he had experienced, until he had forgotten and retrieved it from the depths of his own creative unconscious. The process of meditative recall took place over the course of eighteen critical months immediately after he returned to his native land.

Darwin returned from his five-year voyage to find that his observations and his collections had made him a scientific celebrity.

When he came back, he busied himself cataloguing and distributing the specimens he had sent home during the voyage. He supervised the publication of the scientific report, and wrote up his own **Journal of the Voyage of the Beagle**. This book was to rival Humboldt's **Narrative** as a popular classic of travel.

He also prepared books on the formation of Coral Reefs, on Volcanic Islands and on the Geology of South America. His findings earned him the undying respect of Charles Lyell, and in 1838 he was elected to the secretaryship of the Geological Society.

He was lionized by the intellectual elite of London, and struck up lifelong friendships with scientists who were to become his ardent supporters. The botanist **J.D. Hooker** and, of course, T.H. Huxley.

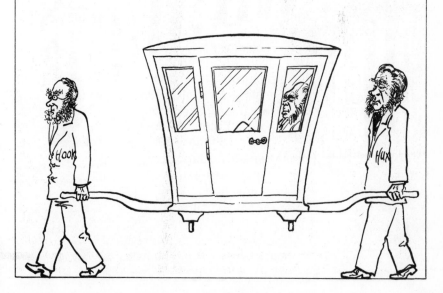

My God, it's intolerable to think of spending one's whole life like a neuter bee, working, working, and nothing after all.—No, no, won't do— imagine living all one's day solitary in smokey dirty London house — only picture to yourself a nice soft wife on a sofa, with a good fire, and books and music perhaps.
Marry—marry— marry. Q.E.D.

The nice soft wife was no sooner pictured than chosen. On November 11th, 1838, Darwin proposed to his cousin **Emma Wedgwood**, and on January 29th, 1839, the wealthy young couple were married and moved into their new house at 12 Upper Gower Street in London.

Like Freud and Marx, Darwin exploited the monotonous security of a happy marriage to work undisturbed at a revolutionary theory. Under the cover of respectable matrimony, all three men succeeded in hatching ideas which did much to undermine the world upon which traditional family life was based.

Darwin's conversion to evolution was well underway by the time he proposed to his young cousin. Emma eventually became reconciled to her husband's ideas; but she would have been shocked to learn what heretical notions he had in his mind on that "day of days" in November 1838! For, a year earlier, Darwin had secretly started the first of several notebooks on the transmutation of species.

While he kept up a public front of traditional belief, he was privately reaching the most dramatically unconventional conclusions. By 1839 these were fully formulated; and in 1842 he allowed himself the satisfaction of sketching out a 35 page outline of what he called "my theory". Two years later, he felt confident enough to expand this sketch into a closely argued essay of 230 pages, and left instructions that it was to be published in the event of his unexpected death.

No doubt, this precaution was prompted by growing anxiety about his own health. In the months following his return, he gradually fell victim to the disabling symptoms which were to plague him for the rest of his life. Less than a year after his marriage, Darwin was so incapacitated by ill health that he withdrew from the social whirl and began to rely on the nursing care provided by his young wife.

He resigned from the secretaryship of the Geological Society, and in 1842 began looking for a quiet rural retreat in which to continue his work. After a prolonged search around London, he found his lifelong home at Down House just outside Sevenoaks. Here he retired into a life of secluded invalidism, working for a few hours each day before surrendering to an ordeal of nausea, weakness, headache and palpitations.

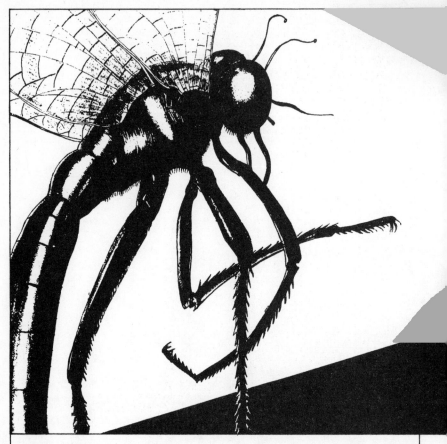

Darwin's illness has always been a subject of controversy. Scientists, reluctant to accept the idea that physical symptoms might have a psychological origin, attribute Darwin's prostration to an infectious disease he picked up on the South American Pampas.

On March 26th, 1835, he "experienced on attack (for it deserves no better name) of the Benchuca, the great black bug of the pampas". It is now known that these insects carry a micro-organism which is responsible for so-called Chagas disease. It seems likely, but not altogether certain, that Darwin was a victim of this disease.

Chagas disease generally has a rapidly fatal outcome. Darwin was seriously disabled by his symptoms, but he had a long and

unexpectedly productive life. He worked much harder than most ordinary people, and enjoyed a happy life with his large family. Curiously, he suffered from many of the same symptoms during the weeks while he was anxiously awaiting the Beagle's departure.

The alternative explanation is that Darwin was crippled by the burden of an overbearing father. It seems quite probable that like many other Victorian intellectuals, both male and female, he was unusually susceptible to psychosomatic illness. One must recognise too that he had to bear the overwhelming strain of incubating an explosively controversial theory. The attack of the Benchuca may have been responsible, but one cannot rule out the possibility that Darwin's ill-health was the result of unremitting anxiety.

Darwin's ideas about nature underwent more change in the months that followed his return than they had during the whole five years of the voyage itself. The voluminous notes he kept during the voyage show little or no evidence of evolutionary thought. Yet, less than eighteen months after he began his 'transmutation' notebooks, his picture of the living world had undergone an irreversible transformation.

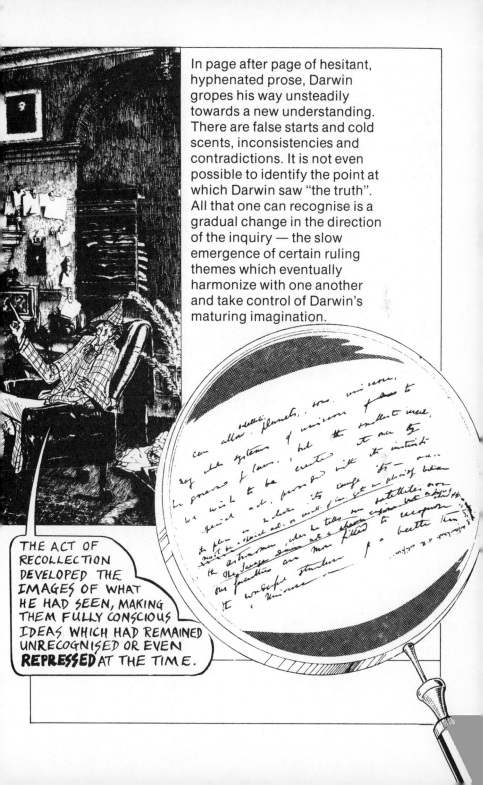

In page after page of hesitant, hyphenated prose, Darwin gropes his way unsteadily towards a new understanding. There are false starts and cold scents, inconsistencies and contradictions. It is not even possible to identify the point at which Darwin saw "the truth". All that one can recognise is a gradual change in the direction of the inquiry — the slow emergence of certain ruling themes which eventually harmonize with one another and take control of Darwin's maturing imagination.

THE ACT OF RECOLLECTION DEVELOPED THE IMAGES OF WHAT HE HAD SEEN, MAKING THEM FULLY CONSCIOUS IDEAS WHICH HAD REMAINED UNRECOGNISED OR EVEN **REPRESSED** AT THE TIME.

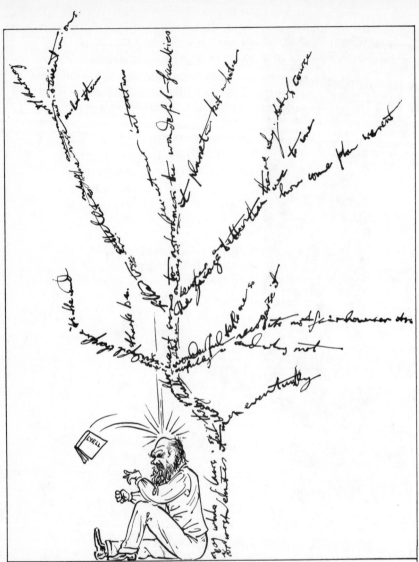

At the time he opened the first notebook in July 1837, Darwin was a convert to Lyell's belief in uniform geological change. He realised this implied a corresponding change in the character of living things. In order to **remain** adapted to their environment, living things must have altered, and in all probability would continue to do so. By the end of 1837, Darwin had come to the conclusion that nature was an open-ended process of **"becoming"**.

Darwin began to appreciate that if the **globe** had undergone such far-reaching changes as Lyell suggested, it was not unreasonable to assume that **life** had undergone a comparable transformation. If not, the passage of time would have brought about a lethal maladjustment between living things and their environment, and in the long run the earth would have depopulated itself.

93

EITHER THEY'VE BEEN SPECIALLY CREATED IN ORDER TO MAKE UP FOR THE LOSSES DUE TO EXTINCTION.

OR

THEY'VE EVOLVED FROM THEIR OUTDATED PRE-DECESSORS.

In contrast to Lyell who refused to admit the possibility of biological change, Darwin rejected the first alternative. In the early pages of his notebooks, he began to explore the possibilities of the second. By the middle of 1837 he was convinced that life had "evolved" and that the emergence of new species was the result of "descent with modification".

At the outset he modelled this process along lines similar to his predecessor, Lamarck. In other words, he visualized biological change as something directly shaped by the alterations in the physical environment, with plants and animals progressively fitting themselves to the changes in the physical world. And like Lamarck, he entertained the possibility of spontaneous generation whereby inanimate matter sprang into life in order to replenish the lower reaches of the ascending escalator.

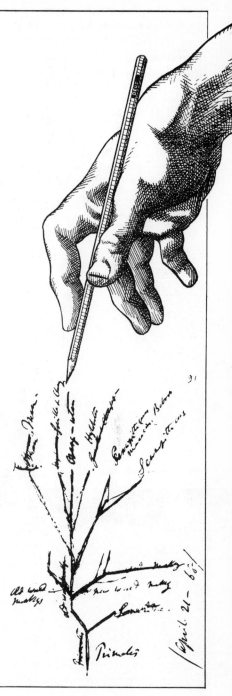

Before long however, he abandoned the idea of spontaneous generation, realizing that evolution was not necessarily a **single** line of ascent. Simple organisms could give rise to more complex ones without necessarily vanishing in the process. This led him to his first significant image. The image of an irregularly branching tree. He drew a diagram in the margin of his notebook to illustrate what he meant.

Each new species establishes itself as new shoots springing off from the parent tree. These shoots branch in their turn, and then divide again and so on — presumably ad infinitum. Shortly afterwards, he suggested

the tree of life should perhaps be called the coral of life, base of branches dead so that passages cannot be seen.

This simple concept neatly explained Darwin's South American findings.

99

The idea of a common forefather was a much more reasonable explanation than the suggestion that there had been a series of ad hoc creations. The same diagram also helped to explain why the fauna of Australia was so different from that of the rest of the world: "countries longest separated — greatest differences — if separated from immense age, but each having its representatives". Darwin recognised that life branched out from a common stem and brought about what we now call **adaptive radiation,** with organisms insinuating themselves into every possible habitat. At this early stage, Darwin knew that he could claim no originality for his theory. Diderot, Lamarck and Erasmus Darwin had all speculated about descent from a common ancestor. And the same principle had been successfully applied to the study of linguistic history. At the end of the 18th century, **Sir William Jones** had drawn attention to the phonetic similarities between certain key words in Latin, Greek and Sanskrit. By 1816, the philologist **Franz Bopp** suggested that all European languages had descended with modification from the same Indo-European root.

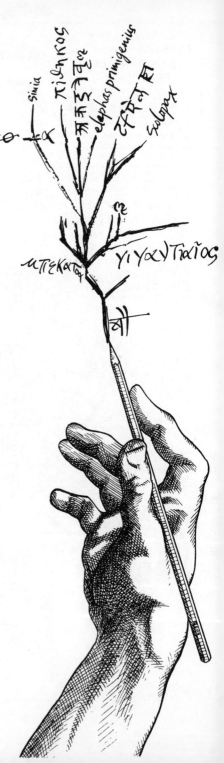

BUT THE THEORY OF DESCENT WITH MODIFICATION DIDN'T GO FAR ENOUGH. FOR, WHILE IT INDICATED THAT BIOLOGICAL CHANGE HAD TAKEN PLACE, IT DIDN'T EXPLAIN HOW OR WHY. DARWIN HAD NOW TO ANSWER TWO QUESTIONS . . . .

HOW IS EVOLUTION PROPELLED?

HOW IS IT DIRECTED?

HOW DID NEW SPECIES EMERGE; AND WHAT GUARANTEED THEIR ADAPTATION?

1. The source of biological change

For want of a better explanation, Darwin began by stipulating that environmental changes were directly responsible for producing biological alterations. This argument went as follows:

(a) Geological changes alter the lie of the land, and this in turn brings about changes in the natural habitat of living things.

(b) In the effort to survive these altered circumstances, living organisms change their habits.

(c) Repeated and long lasting changes in behaviour eventually bring about permanent changes in physical form.

(d) These become stamped into the make-up of living things, and are rendered more or less permanent by being handed on from one generation to the next.

Darwin never altogether abandoned his mistaken belief in the Lamarckian inheritance of acquired characteristics, and throughout his life he continued to believe that the environment was capable of inducing hereditary adaptations.

In the first few pages of his notebook Darwin drew attention to the fact that sexual reproduction invariably gave rise to fortuitous novelties. Although living things characteristically breed true to type, the members of any given species recognisably differ not only from their **parents,** but from **one another** too.

But he was also drawn to an alternative scheme. By 1839 he was convinced that nature provided the raw material for evolution in the shape of **random unsolicited novelties** which sprang into existence without any regard to their biological usefulness.

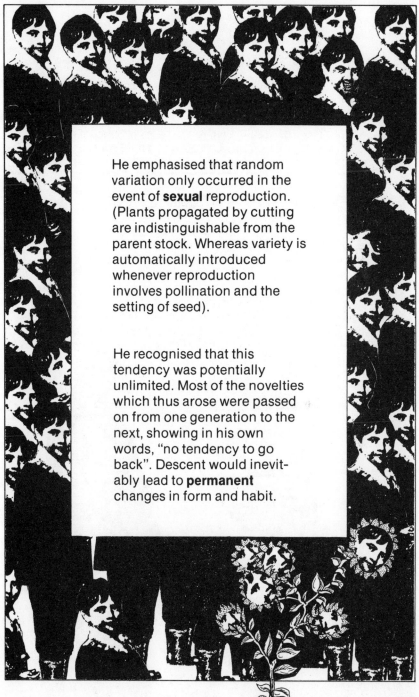

He emphasised that random variation only occurred in the event of **sexual** reproduction. (Plants propagated by cutting are indistinguishable from the parent stock. Whereas variety is automatically introduced whenever reproduction involves pollination and the setting of seed).

He recognised that this tendency was potentially unlimited. Most of the novelties which thus arose were passed on from one generation to the next, showing in his own words, "no tendency to go back". Descent would inevitably lead to **permanent** changes in form and habit.

THE FACT THAT LIVING THINGS HAVE A DEMONSTRABLE TENDENCY TO DEPART FROM THEIR ANCESTRAL FORM DOESN'T NECESSARILY MEAN THAT THEY WILL DEVELOP IN A PROFITABLE DIRECTION.

... ON THE CONTRARY, THE ACCUMULATION OF FORTUITOUS NOVELTY COULD BE JUST AS DANGEROUS AS RIGID IMMUTABILITY, IN FACT, THIS WAS ONE OF THE MAIN REASONS WHY LYELL OBJECTED TO THE IDEA OF BIOLOGICAL CHANGE. RECOGNISING THAT THERE WAS A STRUGGLE FOR EXISTENCE LYELL HAD POINTED OUT THAT ANY DEPARTURE FROM THE WELL ADAPTED FORMS INAUGURATED BY THE CREATOR WOULD SOON BE ELIMINATED.

Darwin used the very same argument to prove that evolution had to take place, and that the struggle for existence provided the directive principle that he was looking for. For although Lyell's argument would have applied to a changeless world, it made no sense in a world which was constantly undergoing physical transformation.

Like many of his predecessors, Darwin was struck by the far-reaching changes which plants and animals had undergone in the course of human domestication. By studying the establishment of these artificial breeds, Darwin succeeded in identifying the principle which directed evolution into profitable channels.

He developed an almost obsessional interest in the work of gardeners, farmers, stock-breeders and pigeon-fanciers. He frequented cattle markets and sales, and immersed himself in agricultural catalogues and horticultural gazettes. He began to realise that the development of new strains was the result of selective breeding.

Unable to induce the improvements which he needs, the stockbreeder is forced to work with the unsolicited novelties which nature provides. All that he can do is to identify promising traits,if and when they appear, and by isolating these fortunate individuals, and by getting them to mate with others of the same sort, he can encourage the development of new and more profitable breeds.

BUT THIS PROCESS INVOLVES A CONSCIOUS **CHOICE** ON THE PART OF THE BREEDER . . .

I AM ANXIOUS TO AVOID IMPUTING ANYTHING OF THAT SORT TO NATURE!

The only plausible alternative to **deliberate** selection was blind **competition** — a mindless force which automatically and unpremeditatedly eliminates the unfit. Like his grandfather Erasmus and many of his other predecessors, Darwin realised that the sheer fertility of nature created a struggle for existence. In such a struggle, any individual lucky enough to inherit a favourable variation would stand a better chance of living long enough to hand on its profitable peculiarity to the next generation.

Although he was well aware of the selective role of competition, Darwin didn't recognise its exclusive importance until he accidentally came across a mathematical argument which opened his eyes to its unremitting intensity.

IN OCTOBER 1838, THAT IS FIFTEEN MONTHS AFTER I HAD BEGUN MY SYSTEMATIC ENQUIRY, I HAPPENED TO READ FOR AMUSEMENT MALTHUS **ON POPULATION**

THOMAS MALTHUS WAS A SCHOOLMASTER ECONOMIST WHOSE MAIN PURPOSE IN PUBLISHING A BOOK ON POPULATION WAS TO ARGUE AGAINST THE INDISCRIMINATE USE OF SOCIAL WELFARE.

NATURE IS SO FECUND THAT ANY CARELESS ATTEMPT TO ALLEVIATE POVERTY WILL ENCOURAGE UNSUPPORTABLE INCREASES IN POPULATION, AND WOULD THUS ONLY EXACERBATE THE SUFFERING IT IS DESIGNED TO RELIEVE. AS FAR AS I'M CONCERNED, NATURE IS UNIMPROVABLE. SOCIAL REFORMERS SHOULD THEREFORE ALLOW EVENTS TO TAKE THEIR INEVITABLE COURSE AND LET WAR, DISEASE AND STARVATION REAP THE SURPLUS.

As an instinctive reformer Darwin was horrified by this heartless policy of **laissez-faire**. At the same time, his scientific curiosity was aroused by the mathematical argument on which it was based.

Malthus pointed out that if population went unchecked, it would go on doubling itself every twenty-five years, increasing by what was known as geometrical progression. This would soon outstrip the modest resources of food, air and water, and as a result there would be a ferocious struggle for existence.

When he saw the principle expressed in these numerical terms, Darwin realised that natural selection was the directive force he was looking for. By the winter of 1838 he had all the ingredients of a working hypothesis. The main steps in his argument can now be summarised as follows:

1. The globe has undergone and is continuing to undergo systematic transformation, which means that life on earth must change in order to survive.

2. Nature provides an unlimited supply of **unsolicited, fortuitous,** and hereditary novelties.

3. The fertility of nature leads to an unremitting struggle for existence.

Conclusion

In such a struggle, individuals endowed with favourable novelties will survive, whereas less fortunate individuals will perish. In spite of the fact that each novelty is more or less negligible, their successive accumulation from one generation to the next will lead to the establishment of changes which are far from negligible.

By the age of thirty, Charles Darwin had achieved the paradoxical result of explaining the development of design in terms of **chance**. By bringing together the equally fortuitous principles of random variation and blind competition, he successfully eliminated any further need for providential action.

The fact that he had a workable theory didn't mean Darwin was ready to publish. In spite of the fact that the main outlines of his revolutionary theory were clearly established by 1839, nearly twenty years went by before the **Origin of Species** appeared in print.

The summary which he sketched in 1842 was too short and too unsupported to merit publication. But the 250 page essay which he wrote in 1844 was well developed.

Why then did he delay for a further fifteen years? The following explanations have been offered.

Fear of Controversy & Persecution

Darwin was well aware of the controversy his theory would arouse. Not simply because it suggested that evolution had occurred, but because the mechanism which he had invoked was contrary to all of the most dearly held beliefs of Victorian Christianity. In his notebook Darwin had grimly reminded himself of the persecution meted out to other scientists who had flouted traditional belief. Though he had no reason to fear physical punishment, his good nature made him anxious to avoid giving offence. This anxiety would have been reinforced by the bitter controversy which had been provoked by the anonymous publication of Robert Chambers' **Vestiges of the Natural History of Creation**

Darwin's Religious Beliefs

Darwin has often been portrayed as a life-long atheist, implying that he had no religious beliefs to embarrass his scientific thought. But although he had abandoned orthodox Christianity by the time he set foot on the Beagle, he maintained some sort of religious belief until the last twenty years of his life.

THE THEOLOGIAN PUSEY ACCUSES YOU OF MOUNTING AN ATTACK ON RELIGION!

BUT WHILE I AM COLLECTING FACTS FOR **THE ORIGIN OF SPECIES,** MY "BELIEF" IN A PERSONAL GOD IS AS FIRM AS THAT OF DR. PUSEY HIMSELF. PERHAPS THAT'S ANOTHER REASON FOR DELAYING PUBLICATION...

OPIUM IS THE RELIGION OF THE MASSES

TAKE A HIT OF ENLIGHTENMENT, FRIEND...

Scientific Caution

The most important factor was Darwin's doubt about the scientific credibility of his own theory. His intellectual upbringing had taught him that unless a theory had been **induced** from observable facts, it was nothing more than a hypothesis, and that as such it had no serious claims for scientific respect. He recognised that evolution could not be observed **directly,** and could only be deduced from indirect evidence. The only way of overcoming this difficulty was to collect such an overwhelming mass of indirect evidence that the deduction would be inescapable. It was nearly twenty years before he had amassed what he regarded as the right amount.

But apart from this methodological scruple Darwin recognised that there was a much more specific objection to his theory. Until he had an answer to it, he would always be vulnerable to criticism.

THE THEORY OF NATURAL SELECTION PRESUPPOSED THE EXISTENCE OF FORTUITOUS VARIATION – AN UNLIMITED TENDENCY TO DEPART FROM THE PARENTAL FORM. ALTHOUGH HE HAD AMPLE EVIDENCE TO SUPPORT HIS BELIEF IN SUCH UNSOLICITED NOVELTIES, HE WAS UNABLE TO EXPLAIN: WHAT CAUSED THEM? WHAT PREVENTED THEM FROM DISSIPATING, ONCE THEY HAD MADE THEIR FIRST APPEARANCE?

Meanwhile he continued to work in the invalid solitude of his country retreat. He continued to collect the evidence he needed to flesh out the theory which he had privately described in 1844. But his published work made no direct reference to the theory of evolution.

In 1846 he published his work on the geology of South America. For the next eight years he devoted himself to a comparative study of barnacles — a group of animals whose relationship to the crustacea (crabs, shrimps and crayfish) had only recently been established.

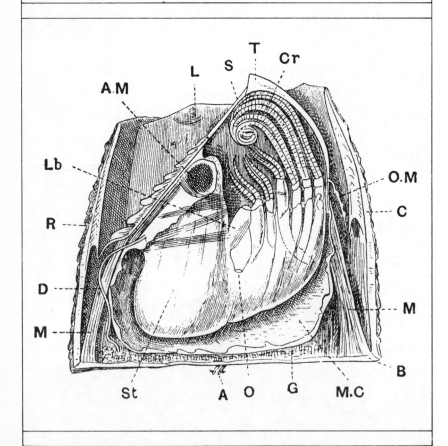

Darwin's interest in this obscure and somewhat unglamorous creature would seem at first sight to have nothing to do with his main line of research. But by accumulating an enormous number of different species he inadvertently reinforced his belief in natural variety. He was able to demonstrate the enormous number of ways in which a basic plan could be modified in order to meet different circumstances. Moreover, the barnacle exhibited the fundamental importance of embryological evidence.

FOR ALTHOUGH THE ADULT FORMS DIFFER FROM ONE ANOTHER TO THE POINT WHERE IT'S SOMETIMES DIFFICULT TO SEE WHY ONE SHOULD REGARD THEM AS MEMBERS OF THE SAME GROUP, THE LARVAL STAGES ARE SO INDISTINGUISHABLE THAT IT'S IMPOSSIBLE TO ESCAPE THE CONCLUSION THAT THEY HAVE ALL DESCENDED FROM A COMMON ANCESTOR.

Darwin published his barnacle books in 1851 and 1854, and returned once more to the work which he had left unfinished ten years previously. By this time his close friends knew about the great work he was incubating. They encouraged him to publish. In 1856 his brother Erasmus warned him that "someone will have been there before you".

On the 14th May, 1856, he began to compile a book which he had intended to call **Natural Selection**. By October he had written two chapters dealing with "Variations under domestication". Early in the New Year he dealt with variation under nature, and by March he had written the chapter dealing with the part played by the struggle for existence. By the middle of 1857 he was exhausted and ill, and went to take the water cure...

His return to work was disastrously interrupted by a coincidence which demonstrated the scientific inevitability of the theory which he had for so many years regarded as his own.

On the 18th June, 1858, he received a letter from a young naturalist, **Alfred Russel Wallace,** who had been working for many years in the Malay Archipelago.

Wallace had written to ask Darwin's advice about a scientific paper which outlined a theory suggesting that natural selection played an essential part in shaping the development of living species. Darwin was thunderstuck and wrote to Lyell to say that he had been forestalled.

IF WALLACE HAD MY MS. SKETCH WRITTEN OUT IN 1842 HE COULD NOT HAVE MADE A BETTER SHORT ABSTRACT! EVEN HIS TERMS NOW STAND AS HEADS IN MY CHAPTERS...

Darwin was in a quandary. Publish or not to publish.

On the 1st July, 1858, Darwin and Wallace published an article in the Journal of the Linnean Society, "On the Tendency of Species to Form Varieties; and On the Perpetuation of Varieties and Species by Natural Means of Selection".

Scientific pioneers are usually portrayed as friendless heroes battling against insuperable odds of mockery and neglect. This sentimental fiction overlooks three important facts.

1. THE PERSUASIVENESS OF A GREAT NEW TRUTH ALMOST INVARIABLY WINS IT SOME REPUTABLE FRIENDS.

2. THE DIVERSITY OF SCIENTIFIC OPINION MEANS THAT THE NUMBER OF PEOPLE PREPARED TO RECOGNISE THE VALUE OF A NEW THEORY IS NEVER NEGLIGIBLE.

3. SCIENTIFIC REVOLUTIONS ARE USUALLY PRECEDED BY A LONG PERIOD OF CONFLICT AND DOUBT, DURING WHICH TIME THE INCONSISTENCIES OF THE TRADITIONAL DOGMA HAVE BEEN WIDELY RECOGNISED. WHEN THE NEW THEORY ARRIVES ON THE SCENE, IT IS OFTEN WELCOMED FOR BRINGING COHERENCE AND INTELLIGIBILITY.

So, far from meeting a wall of opposition, the **Origin of Species** was greeted with relief and enthusiasm by some of the most important scientists in Great Britain. T.H. Huxley blamed himself for not having thought of it before; Wallace, as we've seen, already had; and the botanist J.D. Hooker, once a fervent believer in the permanence of species, was immediately converted by reading the **Origin**.

These three were only the spearhead of Darwin's support. Within a few years the consensus in favour of the new theory had grown to impressive proportions. In any case, by 1859 the fact of evolution was widely accepted, although the mechanism was still in doubt.

Naturally there were sustained objections. But since these were promoted by many different motives, some less creditable than others, they never added up to a concerted opposition. The scientifically illiterate misread the work and didn't know enough biology to recognise the problem. The most notorious expression of this took place in Oxford at the 1860 meeting of the British Association for the Advancement of Science. Puffed up with stupidity and self-satisfaction, Bishop Wilberforce — 'Soapy Sam' to his enemies — made a British ass of himself in the complacent belief that he had destroyed Darwin's intellectual reputation. Less prominent churchmen contented themselves by spreading the rumour that Darwin was the most dangerous man in Europe.

The opposition was not confined to the ranks of the more idiotic clergy, however. Reputable scientists, whose thought was entrenched in traditional Creationism, found it impossible to adjust their vision. Darwin's old teacher Sedgwick was bewildered and disappointed by his pupil's "error", and dreaded the moral implications of extending such a theory to mankind. Agassiz in the United States remained an opponent to the end of his life.

Malice and professional envy also played a part. The comparative anatomist, **Richard Owen,** who knew more than enough biology to recognise the truth, was driven by wounded pride to write a long spiteful article in which he deliberately twisted the facts in an effort to discredit the new theory. Darwin wisely disregarded most of these objections, insisting that he could have written much more damaging criticism himself.

But three objections at least gave him serious trouble.

First objection
The zoologist H. St. George Mivart argued that although natural selection might account for the success of well-established adaptations, it couldn't possibly explain the initial stages of their development. The biological usefulness of the eye is self-evident, but how did such an organ get started in the first place?

IF YOU ARE RIGHT, AND THE BUILDING BLOCKS OF EVOLUTION CONSIST OF VERY SMALL FORTUITOUS NOVELTIES THERE MUST HAVE BEEN A STAGE AT WHICH THE INCIPIENT ORGAN HAD NO RECOGNIZABLE FUNCTION, AND WOULD THERE-FORE HAVE CONFERRED NO SELECTIVE ADVANTAGE. THEREFORE USEFUL ORGANS MUST HAVE DEVELOPED **WITH A VIEW** TO THE FUNCTION THEY WOULD EVENTUALLY SERVE!

We now recognise that Darwin's explanation is true: that, at its first appearance, a fortuitous novelty may confer subtle and invisible advantages. Nevertheless, the "utility" of imperceptible novelties continued to be a problem, and was one of the reasons why natural selection became discredited in Darwin's own lifetime.

Second objection
(THE ABSENCE OF INTERMEDIATE TYPES)

CHARLES! IF YOU GO ON OVERSTRESSING THE IMPORTANCE OF IMPERCEPTIBLE CHANGE AND INSIST ON THE GRADUAL TRANSITION FROM ONE TYPE TO THE NEXT, YOU'LL BE DIGGING YOUR OWN GRAVE!

CHARLES DARWIN R.I.P.

Darwin was well-aware of the fact that there were huge gaps in the fossil record. He explained these by assuming that the intermediate stages had been destroyed. To him, it was as if some geological vandal had torn out pages and chapters in the book of life. But he was confident that subsequent research would restore these lost episodes and that the continuity of the record would eventually be restored.

This has not happened. Modern palaeontologists now recognise that Darwin did not explain the often abrupt succession of fossil types. There is now overwhelming evidence pointing to the conclusion that certain forms remained stable for long periods of time, only to be suddenly succeeded by new forms altogether. Latter-day Creationists have seized on this finding, in the effort to reinstate the doctrine of serial creations. Serious biologists dismiss this as a frivolous suggestion. But they are ready to concede that the process of evolution is more episodic than Darwin supposed. Confronted by the fact of so many unbridgeable gaps in the fossil record, palaeontologists are trying to accommodate themselves to the idea that the modification which accompanies descent is not necessarily gradual. Whilst the process of imperceptible change has an all-important part to play in the origin of species, it is often superseded by abrupt transformations which result in the emergence of comprehensively new designs.

The exact mechanism of these rapid changes is now a subject of heated controversy. One biologist has described these novelties as "hopeful monsters", and has argued that an unsolicited transformation in the genetic instructions might occasionally result in the emergence of a design fortuitously adapted to the new circumstances, thrown up at a time of rapid geological change. Although this suggestion kills two birds with one stone, since it deals (a) with the apparent absence of intermediate types, and (b) the apparent uselessness of incipient novelties, it presupposes disruptively large changes in the hereditary instructions. Modern geneticists argue that such abrupt upheavals would prove lethally disabling to the process of embryological development. Whatever the explanation is, it must eventually account for the fact that evolution has not always been a smooth process, and that the history of life on earth has often been sharply punctuated.

Third objection

An evolutionary theory which is based on the slow accumulation of small invisible novelties presupposes huge lengths of time. As we've already seen, the geologists of the 18th and 19th centuries had gradually recognised the great age of the earth. But Darwin's theory demanded an almost inconceivable span of biological time. This assumption was seriously endangered when the physicist **Lord Kelvin** calculated from the temperature of the earth's interior that Darwin had grossly overestimated the age of the globe.

Darwin rightly suspected that Kelvin's calculation would turn out to be wrong. If he'd lived longer, he would have been gratified to discover that the earth was even older than he supposed.

The Fourth Objection

Darwin's ignorance about the mechanism of inheritance left him exposed to an even more damaging objection. In 1867 a Scottish engineer called **Fleeming Jenkin** pointed out that a favourable variation would soon disperse itself as the 'fortunate' individual interbred with 'normal' members of the population.

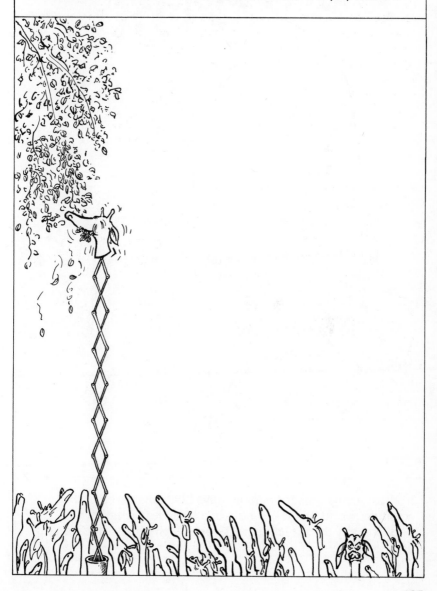

Jenkin's objection was based on the assumption that the genetic factors were infinitely divisible, which implied that a new variation would automatically distribute itself in steadily **diminishing** amounts.

Ironically, this objection could have been answered, if the scientific world had taken note of a discovery which was published by the Czech monk **Gregor Mendel,** less than a year after Jenkin.

Working in the obscurity of a provincial monastery, Mendel proved that the genetic factors behaved as if they were **indivisible** particles, and that they did not blend or dilute themselves in the course of interbreeding. Unfortunately, Mendel's paper was neglected, and by the time it was rediscovered in 1900, the theory of small unsolicited novelties had undergone a total eclipse.

WELL SEE MORE OF THIS MENDEL LATER...

Confronted by the twin spectres of Kelvin and Jenkin, Darwin began to lose confidence in the effectiveness of natural selection. He now felt it necessary to introduce some auxiliary process which would hasten evolutionary change in a purposive direction.

In summarising the sixth and final edition of the **Origin of Species,** he conceded that natural selection was:

". . . aided in an important manner by the inherited effects of the use and disuse of parts; and in an unimportant manner, that is in relation to adaptive structures, whether past or present, by the direct action of external conditions . . . It appears that I formerly underrated the frequency and value of these latter forms of variation, as leading to permanent modifications of structure independently of natural selection."

By introducing this codicil, Darwin reverted to his original belief in the Lamarckian hereditary effect of effort and experience. In 1868 he published a two volume book containing an elaborate theory which purported to explain the inheritance of acquired characteristics.

The Theory Of Pangenesis

By the middle of the 19th century, it was recognised that the only material link between one generation and the next was the fertilised cell which resulted from the fusion of sperm and ovum. From this tiny speck of matter, a new individual was reconstituted in the image of its parents. But no-one could explain how such a small entity could contain all the necessary specifications.

In his **Theory of Pangenesis,** Darwin formulated a theory which was very similar to one which had been put forward by the Ancient Greek Philosopher Democritus. According to this theory, the cells destined to play a reproductive role gradually accumulate a set of representative particles, or "gemmules", derived from all the organs and tissues of the adult body.

Democritus

It was as if the body were divided into a series of parliamentary constituencies, each one of which sent a team of representatives commissioned to reproduce the limbs, organs or tissues for which they stood. These gemmules were dispatched into the blood stream; and having reassembled in the reproductive cells, their presence guaranteed a faithful reduplication of the parent physique.

For Darwin, this theory proved an admirable explanation for the inheritance of acquired characteristics. If, through its own efforts, a creature succeeded in enlarging the muscles of its limbs, the number of gemmules arising from these overgrown parts would increase, and they would therefore be over-represented in the constituent assembly gathered in the reproductive cells. The offspring would therefore automatically inherit the fruits of its parents' exertion.

Conversely, if a limb or organ dwindled through disuse, the gemmules would be under-represented, and the offspring would inherit the parental deficit. This revision gave heart to those who already suspected the evolutionary role of unsolicited variation; and the fact that Darwin himself had made such a concession was one of the factors which led to the development of a Lamarckian backlash. From 1870 the revision gathered momentum, and in the years shortly before Darwin's death there was a veritable landslide in favour of Lamarck.

In Europe and in the United States, evolution was widely accepted as a doctrine, but natural selection was rejected in favour of:
(a) The inherited effects of use and disuse.
(b) The hereditary effects stimulated directly by the environment.

By the end of the century, only two important scientists were prepared to regard unsolicited variation as the raw material of evolutionary change. Both of them remained unswervingly loyal to the principle of natural selection. Alfred Russel Wallace and the German naturalist August Weismann.

Weismann's Neo~Darwinism

According to Weismann the doctrine of the inheritance of acquired characteristics was factually wrong and biologically impossible.

BEFORE AFTER NOTYET

After sifting all the experimental evidence Weismann was unable to find a single case in which the experience and effort of one generation had influenced the structure and function of the next. Experimental scars and mutilations were never inherited. Nor were skills. The brawny muscles acquired by a blacksmith during a lifetime of toil were not handed on to his idle son. Regardless of the changes undergone during the lifetime of any one individual, the next generation invariably reverted to type.

Weismann explained this by drawing a contrast between the perishable cells of the body and the 'immortal' cells responsible for reproduction. In a paper published in 1883 he pointed out that the cells which participate in **adaptive** change perish with the death of the individual, and cannot therefore bequeath the results of effort and experience to the next generation. The only cells which survive the death of the individual are the ones destined to play a reproductive role.

Since these cells are segregated at an early stage in development, their genetic capability remains unaffected by the changes undergone by the rest of the body.

According to Weismann, the perishable generations are linked to one another by an imperishable line of hereditary material. The inviolable continuity of this immortal 'germ plasm' prevents the transmission of characteristics acquired during the lifetime of any one individual.

The Central Dogma

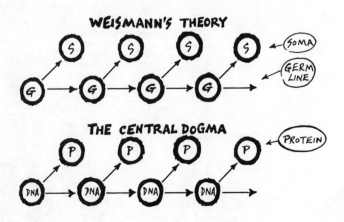

WEISMANN'S THEORY

SOMA

GERM LINE

THE CENTRAL DOGMA

PROTEIN

THE STRUCTURE OF DNA (DEOXYRIBONUCLEIC ACID).

A: ADENINE ; T: THYMINE ⎫
C: CYTOSINE ; G: GUANINE ⎬ THE FOUR BASES

r: RIBOSE SUGAR; p: PHOSPHATE WHICH TOGETHER FORM THE BACKBONE
OF EACH STRAND.

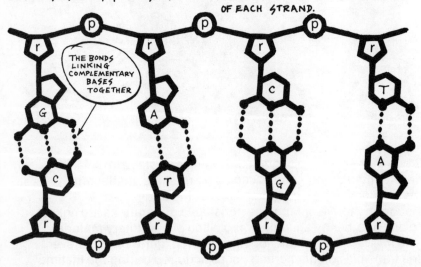

THE BONDS LINKING COMPLEMENTARY BASES TOGETHER

THE REPLICATION OF DNA

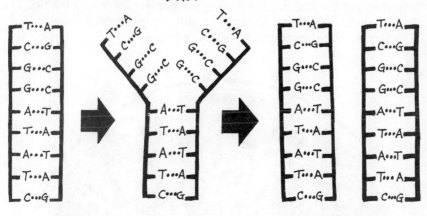

With the discovery of nuclear DNA, Weismann's theory was translated into the *Central Dogma* of modern genetics.

The genetic instructions are conveyed from one generation to the next in the form of a linear programme which is digitally coded throughout the length of a self-replicating molecule of DNA.

This code dictates the synthesis of many different proteins, and the orderly interaction of these secondary products culminates in the characteristic form and function of the adult organism.

But the outcome is not rigidly determined. Within certain limits, the process is modified by the environment – temperature, nutrition, exertion etc. – so that the final form of the adult body represents the interaction of *invariable* genetic instructions and the *changeable* circumstances within which those instructions are carried out.

But since the biochemical information flows in one direction only, the DNA inherited from the parents remains unaffected by the experiences and exertions of the offspring.

147

By 1885 Weismann identified the nucleus of the germ cell as a carrier of **genetic information**. When biologists observed the nucleus of the sperm penetrating the nucleus of the ovum, he concluded that male and female made equal contributions to the genetic endowment of the fertilized egg.

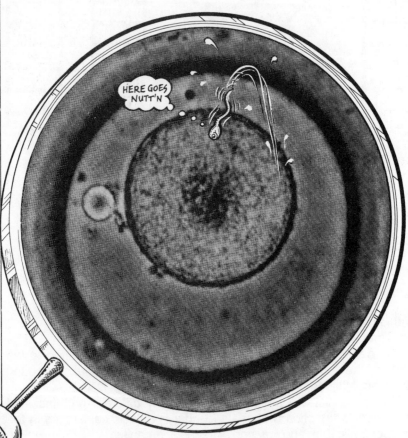

Weismann went on to analyse this dual bequest, and came to the conclusion that it was made up of separate units, or 'determinants'. Breeding experiments had already convinced him that the characteristics of the organism could vary independently of one another, and that they could be separately transmitted. And from this he deduced the **separable, particulate** character of the genetic material.

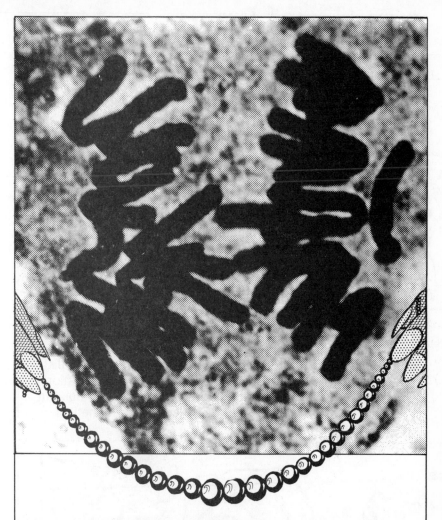

By the end of the century, improvements in microscopy had shown that the nuclear substance was organised into a discrete set of small solid threads, or **chromosomes**. Later work showed that the hereditary factors were strung along the length of these threads, like beads on a necklace.

Weismann's work set the stage for the rediscovery of Mendel's long-forgotten work. In 1900 three biologists independently realized the neglected significance of the Czech monk's experiments.

Gregor Mendel's Discovery

Mendel is often portrayed as the pioneer of mathematical genetics. But he was not the first scientist to analyse heredity in quantitative terms. In the 18th century, the German naturalist Kohlreuter carried out a large series of trials on hybridization and obtained results which forshadowed those of Mendel. But these experiments were hampered by lack of mathematical rigour.

Mendel superseded this work by recognising the deep logical structure of inheritance, and by designing experiments which would display this in an easily manageable symbolic notation.

By choosing characteristics which differed from one another in an unmistakable fashion, he was able to represent their presence or absence in an all-or-none manner. And since this allowed him to use a binary notation, his calculations were formal and unambiguous.

He chose a plant which exhibited clearly contrasted **pairs** of characteristics, and allocated an alphabetical symbol for each one. He observed that the garden pea could be readily sorted into two separate types. There were tall plants and short ones — and no intermediate form to blur the distinction. Some of the plants had yellow peas, others had green ones etc., etc. In each of his experiments he followed the fate of one of these contrasted pairs, as the plants underwent cross pollination.

For example, he chose a pure strain of tall peas (i.e. peas which invariably gave birth to tall offspring when they were self-fertilized) and cross-pollinated them with a pure strain of the dwarf variety.

All the members of this hybrid generation were tall, and the fact that there were no intermediate examples convinced him that the genetic factor determining height was conveyed in the form of an indivisible unit — one unit for 'dwarf' — another unit for 'tall'. For reasons which he was unable to explain, the tall factor was **dominant,** and somehow prevented the expression of the alternative, so-called **recessive** factor.

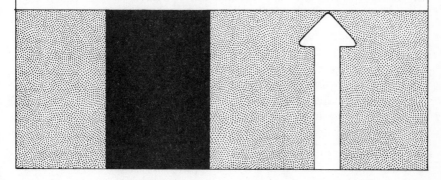

From these results, Mendel might have concluded that the 'dwarf' factor had been destroyed. But his next experiment proved that it was indestructible. For when he interbred or self-fertilized the members of these apparently tall hybrids, he obtained a mixed crop of tall and dwarf plants in the sharp ratio of 3:1.

In order to explain the unexpected reappearance of the dwarf variety, Mendel postulated that the 'dwarf' factor survived its partnership with the 'tall' one, but that it was only able to re-express itself when paired with a recessive factor of the same type. His symbolic notation allowed him to represent the process as a straightforward system of permutations and combinations. According to Mendel, the germ cells contributed by each of the parents could contain two possible genetic combinations.

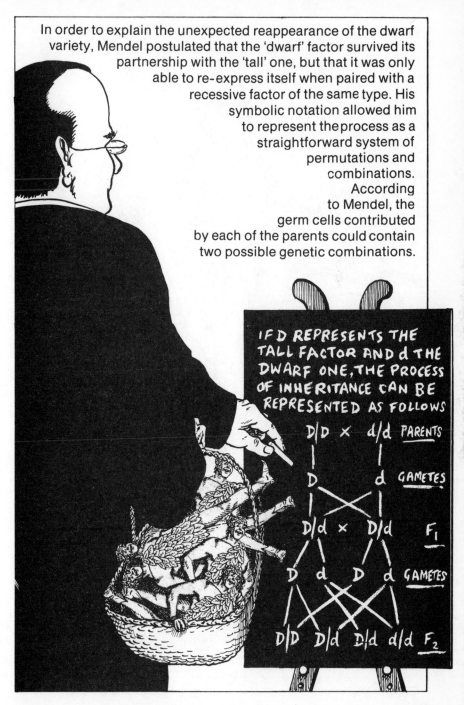

IF D REPRESENTS THE TALL FACTOR AND d THE DWARF ONE, THE PROCESS OF INHERITANCE CAN BE REPRESENTED AS FOLLOWS

$D/D \times d/d$ PARENTS

$D \qquad d$ GAMETES

$D/d \times D/d$ F_1

$D \quad d \quad D \quad d$ GAMETES

$D/D \quad D/d \quad D/d \quad d/d$ F_2

155

Mendel's conclusion annihilated Jenkin's objection that genetic novelties would **blend** with interbreeding. And the fact that a characteristic could vanish altogether when crossed with a dominant one, only to reappear in the next generation, showed that the appearance of an individual was not necessarily a guide to its genetic structure. Or as modern geneticists would say, the **Phenotype** is not necessarily a picture of the underlying **Genotype**. The genetic endowment of a given individual can only be displayed by cashing it out in a series of further "crosses". The distinction between **Phenotype** and **Genotype,** i.e., the contrast between the appearance of an individual and its underlying genetic structure was to become a fundamental concept in the evolutionary biology of the 20th century.

Mutation

Paradoxically, the rediscovery of Mendelian genetics in 1900 resulted in a further decline of Darwin's reputation. For although it overcame the difficulties of blending and dilution, it seemed to offer a misleading alternative to Darwin's theory of imperceptible novelties.

In his effort to simplify his analysis, Mendel deliberately chose characteristics which differed from one another in an all-or-none fashion — tall plants versus short plants, yellow peas versus green ones. Geneticists who rediscovered his work assumed that new characteristics would leap into existence with comparable discontinuity, i.e., that when a novelty did occur, by substituting an old gene for a new one, it would express itself as a drastic difference. Evolution was now explained in terms of **mutation**, i.e., by abrupt changes in the genotype which brought about correspondingly large changes in the phenotype. As one geneticist expressed it: "New species are produced from

existing forms by certain leaps." For the Mendelian geneticists, each organism was at the mercy of its random mutations, and evolution was visualized as a staccato sequence of abrupt transformations.

Family Portraits

GREAT GRAND FATHER

GREAT GRAND GLORIOUS FATHER

NANNA & GRANDPA

AUNT FLO

UNCLE BEN

GREAT UNCLE WILBERFORCE

MUM & DAD

Mutation vs. Variation

The idea that biological change jumped from one stage to the next had obvious appeal for scientists who doubted the selective advantage of imperceptible novelties.

For nearly thirty years, there was a deadlock between Mendelian geneticists who visualized evolution as a series of drastic **mutations**, and naturalists who continued to uphold the Darwinian doctrine of continuous **variation**. For the mutationists, natural selection was a negligible influence. But for the Darwinian biologists, who had an eye for what went on in the wild, natural selection was the guiding principle of evolution.

After 1930, a slow reconciliation took place. The result, now called the **New Synthesis**, reinstated Darwin's original theory on a firm foundation of experimental genetics and population statistics. The paradoxical result is that biological opinion is now closer to Darwin than it has been at any other time since the publication of **The Origin of Species**.

The Darwinian Revolution became a convenient but misleading name for a major upheaval in human thought. The mid-point of this revolution coincided with the publication of the **Origin of Species** in 1859. But we have traced its beginnings to the early years of the 18th century. Its full implications did not become apparent until the middle years of this one.

Charles Darwin is usually credited with the heroic, single-handed discovery of evolution. Indispensable contributions were made by people now regarded as befogged predecessors. In the years that followed the **Origin of Species**, Darwin's own work had to be corrected and modified.

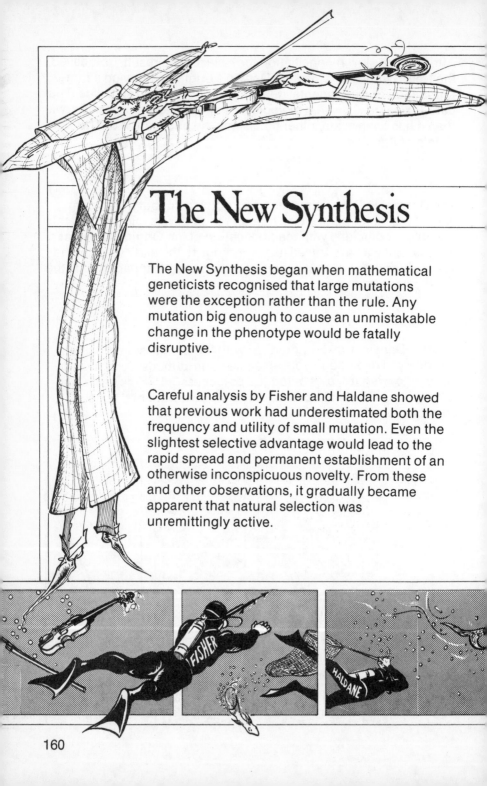

The New Synthesis

The New Synthesis began when mathematical geneticists recognised that large mutations were the exception rather than the rule. Any mutation big enough to cause an unmistakable change in the phenotype would be fatally disruptive.

Careful analysis by Fisher and Haldane showed that previous work had underestimated both the frequency and utility of small mutation. Even the slightest selective advantage would lead to the rapid spread and permanent establishment of an otherwise inconspicuous novelty. From these and other observations, it gradually became apparent that natural selection was unremittingly active.

Further work showed that mutation was by no means the only source of biological novelty. The recombination of existing factors was just as productive as the substitution of new ones. It soon became apparent that the population as a whole represented a bottomless reservoir of variation. Even without mutation, the re-patterning of the genotype which takes place under the auspices of sexual reproduction provides an almost inexhaustible source of genetic novelty.

The geneticists who adopted the Mendelian model of heredity overlooked this by making the useful, but finally unrealistic, assumption that there was a one-to-one relationship between each genetic factor and the bodily characteristic for which it was responsible. Or to put it in mathematical terms, they assumed that

the genotype could be mapped on to the phenotype item for item, like this:

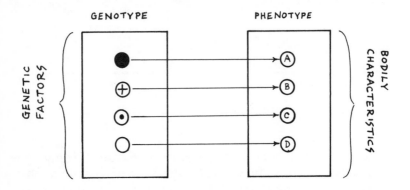

In this situation, there is an arithmetical limit to the number of variations which can be produced by mating different individuals, and no opportunity for transcendent novelty.

By 1950 it was generally recognised that the relationship between genetic factors and bodily characteristics was much more complicated than the Mendelian geneticists supposed. Although the genotype is made up of units which behave as separable bits during the process of reproduction, the pattern that is reassembled in the fertilized egg acts in concert so that it is not possible to draw a straight line from any one determinant to its corresponding feature in the phenotype.

The point is that the molecular sequences of **DNA** which together make up the genetic code do not represent characteristics on a one-to-one basis. In fact, they don't really specify characteristics as such. Each 'bit' of DNA dictates the synthesis of a particular protein, and it is the interaction of all these particular proteins which culminates in the distinctive structure and function of the fully developed adult.

So, when a modern geneticist refers to a gene 'for' a particular characteristic — red eyes, wrinkled seed-coat or whatever — he means that other things being equal, an organism **with** this gene is more likely to display the character in question than an organism without it. But since the protein produced by that gene interacts with the proteins produced by many, if not all, of the others, the presence of that particular factor in the genotype may also be responsible for the development of other features.

For this reason the contribution which any particular gene makes to the fitness of a given individual cannot be assessed in terms of single characteristics. The genotype works as a co-adapted whole, and the utility of any one gene depends on the extent to which it fits in and improves the expression of all the other genes with which the lottery of sexual reproduction has associated it.

For the same reason the evolutionary fate of a mutation, i.e. the substitution of a brand-new gene, depends to a large extent on how the newcomer harmonizes with the pre-existing pattern. Any

beneficial effect which it confers must be offset against the detrimental modifications which it might inflict on the expression of all the other genes.

But even without mutation, the intervention of sexual reproduction guarantees an inescapable measure of emergent novelty, and the tendency to depart from the ancestral form is built in to the very mechanism by which living things purchase their immortality.

In recognising the creative role of sexual reproduction, biologists established a new picture of evolution. Because so much variation is mediated by the process of mating, evolution is bound to be characterised as a collective process, indivisibly shared by the members of an interbreeding population. For although it's the individual whose phenotype must undergo the competitive tests of fitness and utility, it is the network of sexual partnerships which repeatedly generates the relevant novelties.

For modern-biologists, therefore, evolutionary interest has shifted from the individual to the **population** — or to be more accurate, to the reproductive community within which any one member can mate with any other. The population can therefore be represented as a creative entity in its own right — a bounded pool of genes within which each individual should be regarded as a short-lived receptacle holding a small but representative sample of the pool's contents.

164

In the light of this idea, the traditional concept of the species has undergone an irreversible change.

For the biologists of the 17th and 18th centuries the concept of species was essentially 'typological', i.e. organisms — plants and animals — sorted themselves out into natural 'kinds'. Each 'kind' consisted of a group of individuals exhibiting a particular sort of 'privileged sameness'. Or to put it in logical terms, each species constituted a 'set' within which membership was defined (a) by the extent to which the individuals resembled one another, and (b) by the extent to which they could all be distinguished from individuals which differed too much to be included in the set in question.

For the naturalists and geneticists who created the New Synthesis, the criterion of physical distinctiveness was replaced by that of reproductive isolation. In other words, the species is no longer defined as a set of individuals sharing the same morphological characteristics, but as a reproductive confederacy within the boundaries of which there is a free-flow of genes, and on the frontiers of which there are considerable obstacles to such an exchange.

The concept of reproductive isolation is often confused with the notion of inter-specific sterility. But it is now recognised that these are not synonymous terms, and that it is sometimes possible to obtain fertile hybrids between members of otherwise distinct species. What keeps species reproductively distinct is not so much

HMM... NOT OF OUR SET...

their mutual sterility as the existence of isolating mechanisms which create more or less insuperable obstacles to their mating. Such mechanisms can be regarded as prohibitive tariffs which define the frontiers of a customs union or common market.

Isolating Mechanisms

1. Geographical separation.
In species which occupy different geographical areas — so-called allopatric species, the obstacles are self evident. Distance, mountain barriers, and wide stretches of ocean effectively prevent mating.

2. Species which occupy the same geographical area — sympatric species — can also be reproductively isolated.
   (a)   Because they breed at different seasons.
   (b)   Because they occupy mutually exclusive habitats within the same area.

Potential mates may encounter one another, but do not copulate because they are behaviourally incompatible. Potential partner A fails to recognise the ritual mating-signals of partner B, so the fuck's off.

Copulation may be attempted, but there may be a mechanical obstacle which prevents the successful transfer of sperm.

When all these mechanisms fail, there may be additional bars to the success of inter-specific crosses; i.e. successful copulation may occur, the sperm may be transferred, but fertilization is prevented by:

1. Sperm death due to biochemical incompatibility.
2. Successful penetration of the sperm is followed by the immediate death of the fertilized egg.

Finally, there is absolute sterility.

Once these isolating mechanisms have been established, the integrity of the species is self-perpetuating. Sympatric forms can then co-exist in the same geographical area without any risk of losing their specific distinctiveness. For any given species, however, the free-flow of genes which takes place within the reproductive community effectively prevents further differentiation. The only way in which a new species can arise is by introducing geographical separation; after which, the two segregated moieties will naturally evolve to the point where they will develop mutually exclusive reproductive habits. For example, if members of a well-established mainland species drift or migrate to an offshore island, the intervening stretch of ocean will effectively separate the two populations. After a certain length of time, the cumulative effects of mutation and recombination will result in differences culminating in reproductive incompatibility. So that when and if the two populations are re-introduced to one another, their respective members will no longer regard each other as potential mates, and two species will have emerged in the place of the original one.

As soon as they recognised the over-riding importance of reproductive isolation, biologists discovered that each species could exemplify several distinct morphological types. Within a large reproductively isolated population, within which there is a free-flow of genes, it is often possible to distinguish several morphological sub-sets, consistently differing from one another as far as their bodily characteristics are concerned, but nonetheless willing to regard each other as potential mates. Species which display such morphological sub-sets are known as poly-typic species. As Darwin recognised, the various sub-species which make up such a group can be regarded as new species in the making, only requiring geographical separation to confirm the distinction.

Conversely, organisms which are morphologically indistinguishable often turn out to be reproductively incompatible, and for that reason naturalists recognise them as distinct so-called sibling species. In fact once their reproductive incompatibility has been clearly recognised, closer examination often reveals inconspicuous but important morphological differences. For example, in a population of Caribbean fireflies, which were previously thought to constitute a single species, careful analysis revealed the existence of several reproductively distinct sub-groups, and although these groups were previously regarded as morphologically indistinguishable, it was later shown that each group displayed consistently distinctive flashing patterns.

Species is thus a dynamic entity, holding in its collective constitution the ever present possibility of further change. It is to all intents and purposes a super-individual, exemplifying two complementary tendencies. On the one hand it displays INVARIANCE; i.e. by virtue of its hereditary mechanism it tends to preserve and perpetuate a certain standard form. But on the other hand, it displays an unavoidable tendency to vary or depart from this form, through the random intervention of mutation and genetic recombination. Both tendencies are indispensable for the survival of life on earth. Organisms which promiscuously dispersed the hard-won bequests of their predecessors would soon lose their adaptive grip. On the other hand, organisms which slavishly reproduced the structure of their ancestors would soon lose their competitive place in a changing world. It is natural selection which strikes the balance between obstinate conservatism and careless mutability.

By thinking in terms of populations rather than individuals, biologists of the New Synthesis began to reappraise the role of natural selection. Darwin adopted, but never actually coined the phrase 'Survival of the Fittest'. The concept of natural selection as a destructive agency soon gained a foothold on the scientific imagination, and this was one of the reasons why it fell out of favour. It gradually became apparent, however, that the influence was much subtler, and that it was really a question of differential reproduction rather than differential survival, and that what counted was not so much the life or death of certain individuals, but the extent to which any particular type could outbreed its competitors. In other words, the success of a given genotype is to be measured by the amount of representation which that genotype

achieves in the next and in all subsequent generations, remembering of course, that selection never works on genotypes as such, but only upon the phenotypes which express them.

After more than one hundred and twenty years the revolution initiated by Darwin has been reinstated and irreversibly confirmed.

Darwin's vision of biological change was so comprehensive that man was unavoidably implicated. But it was more than ten years before Darwin dared to say so explicitly. Reading between the lines of **The Origin of Species** it is easy to tell that Darwin included the human pedigree in the developing tree of life. In 1871 he openly committed himself to describing the descent of man, and in a companion volume on the expression of the emotions, he demonstrated that human behaviour could be traced back to its ancestral origins in animal snarls. From then on man could be no longer regarded as a divine steward, specially created to supervise and exploit God's natural handiwork. Man, the paragon of purposiveness and foresight, was one amongst a number of mechanisms whose peculiar efficiency was the product of chance and necessity.

Unfortunately the term **natural selection** has been misunderstood and abused, and is still criticized for implications which Darwin never intended.

1. By using the word selection, Darwin opened himself to the objection that he had re-introduced the notion of deliberate choice. Nothing could be further from the truth. By drawing an analogy between the selective breeding exercised by man and the competitive pressure exerted by nature, Darwin didn't imply the existence of any **conscious** process.

2. Some of Darwin's more foolish critics point out that the notion of 'survival of the fittest' is a circular argument: whatever is fit is bound to survive and anything which survives is bound to be fit. But Darwin only adopted the slogan at the suggestion of Herbert Spencer and meant it to be interpreted as follows. Given the unremitting competition for food, space and mates, certain variations confer a natural advantage. As long as these favourable variations are heritable they will automatically increase in frequency from one generation to the next.

Spencer's slogan backfired for another somewhat different reason. It gave the misleading impression that natural selection was an elimination contest. Since nature favoured the strong and exterminated the weak, human affairs would be more efficient if they were conducted on the same principle. This led to a regrettable idiocy known as **Social Darwinism**, according to which the ruthless economic competition displayed by capitalism should be encouraged in order to obtain an efficiency comparable to the one exhibited in nature.

In the light of modern genetics Darwin's theory can be re-expressed as follows.

The structure and function of any particular organism represents the culmination of a developmental process in which a group of hereditary factors or genes dictate the synthesis of proteins. The interaction of these various proteins within a given environment — and by environment is meant such variables as climate, nutrition, etc. — leads to a characteristic appearance and behaviour called the phenotype.

But the genotype of any one individual represents a small sample of the factors which are present within a single interbreeding population. Within such a population many genes exist in several alternative forms, and the presence of one rather than another will cause slight but noticeable differences in the development of the individual concerned. The result is that the individuals which make up a population will always differ from one another, although these differences will tend to cluster around a mean or average.

Given the struggle for food and mates, the alternative versions of each variable gene are constantly competing with one another for representation in the next generation. Any gene which confers a selective advantage on the individual endowed with it will tend to make more surviving copies of itself than any of its competing alternatives.

So that although natural selection acts on the survival and reproductive success of individual organisms, what changes during the course of evolution is the relative frequency of genes within a given population. The same process applies to the emergence of man. Though Darwin was unaware of the genetic process involved, he recognised at a very early stage that there was no way of exempting mankind from the evolutionary process which he had described. In 1871, after postponing what he knew would be a controversial conclusion, he made it clear that man too was nothing more than a modified descendant of mammalian ancestors. He did not state,as is so often and carelessly said, that man descended from the monkeys, but that man and monkeys were modified descendants of a primate predecessor.

Even today there are those who find this conclusion quite unacceptable, and in recent years there have been last ditch attempts to reinstate some, indeed any, alternative to the Darwinian theory of evolution. But the death of Darwin has been greatly exaggerated. While there are still a large number of technical details which remain puzzling, Darwin's theory remains the only plausible account of life on earth. The paradox is that the selective process which encouraged and enhanced the development of human intelligence endowed its owner with a curious reluctance to recognise that he owed his origin to a process which was altogether different from the way in which he planned and designed his own affairs.

The recent revival of Creationist controversy shows that human beings are curiously reluctant to give up the notion of providential purpose. There are still many people who experience a sense of cosmic despair when confronted by the idea that life on earth is the outcome of an unsupervised process of chance and necessity. Some ten years before Darwin published *The Origin of Species*, the poet Tennyson had expressed this anxiety as a result of reading Robert Chambers. The most fanatical opposition, now gathering momentum in England and the United States, shows this anxiety is deep-seated and long-lasting.

Such fears have been exacerbated by crude and often unintelligent reductionism on the part of certain biologists who make too much of the fact that human nature is founded on biological imperatives. By insisting that man has inherited inflexible and undeniable patterns of aggression and competitiveness, simple-minded publicists have given wide currency to the notion that the characteristic virtues of the human race are a mere delusion, and that human affairs are more efficiently conducted on the assumption that our ancestors have bequeathed us an insuperable tendency to be aggressive, acquisitive, and territorially ambitious. Such an analysis, however, overlooks the creative versatility of consciousness, and although this itself can be traced back to selectively determined antecedents in the early history of the human species, the biological pedigree of human nature does not pre-empt the possibility of free will and moral dignity. With the emergence of language and writing, human beings have acquired a constitution which cannot be reduced to a straightforward exchange of signals between biological robots. And if the human race is to retain its confidence and dignity, it cannot do so by denying its descent, but by affirming and consolidating those features which distinguish it from the rest of nature.

FURTHER READING

The literature on Darwin is over-whelmingly large, but the following books are a useful supplement.

Darwin's *Autobiography* (Oxford University Press, 1974) provides a charming introduction, and for those who feel daunted by the full text of *The Origin of Species* (Penguin), *The Illustrated Origin*, abridged and introduced by Richard E. Leakey (Faber, 1979) is an admirable substitute.

Loren Eiseley's *Darwin Century* (Gollancz, 1957) paints a vivid picture, as does the comprehensive biography *Darwin* by Adrian Desmond and James Moore (Michael Joseph, 1991), and these can be supplemented by the first-class series of essays edited by Bentley Glass, *Forerunners of Darwin 1745-1859* (Johns Hopkins Press, 1959).

Ernst Mayr is one of the greatest authorities on evolutionary theory, and although they sometimes make hard reading, his *Evolution and the Diversity of Life* (Belknap: Harvard University Press, 1976) and *Animal Species and Evolution* (Harvard University Press, 1963) provide unrivalled accounts of many aspects of this difficult subject. Stephen Jay Gould's essays are also authoritative, but are readily accessible to the lay-person – *Ever since Darwin* (Penguin, 1981) and *The Panda's Thumb* (Norton, 1980). Richard Dawkins' controversial work *The Selfish Gene* (Oxford University Press, 1989), as long as one regards the title as a polemical metaphor, provides a useful picture of the way evolutionary thought has developed since the discovery of DNA. François Jacob's books on evolution, *The Logic of Life* and *The Possible and the Actual* (Pantheon Books, New York, 1982) are excellent and clear.

Most of the books mentioned above echo the conventional, not to say 'conservative', approach which I have deliberately adopted in the effort to make this difficult subject accessible to the beginner. It could be argued that I have culpably overlooked the social implications of evolutionary thought. As a corrective, I advise the reader to consult some progressive sources, e.g. *Images of the Earth* edited by L.J. Jordanova and Roy S. Porter (Chalfont St. Giles: British Society for the History of Science, 1979) and Robert M. Young's many articles. Useful discussion can be found in the Open University, *Beliefs in Science: An Introduction*.

Jonathan Miller studied natural sciences at Cambridge University and subsequently qualified as a Doctor of Medicine in 1959. After working as a pathologist in Cambridge, he took up a research fellowship in the History of Medicine at University College, London. Since then, he has become well known in Britain, Europe and America as a writer and a director of plays and operas. He is also known for his television series on the history of medicine, *The Body in Question* and his pop-up book, *The Human Body*.

Borin Van Loon is also the illustrator of *Introducing Mathematics, Sociology, Cultural Studies, Buddha, Genetics, Eastern Philosophy* and *Media Studies*. He is a surrealist artist whose work ranges from oil paintings to a cut-out book on DNA.

Index